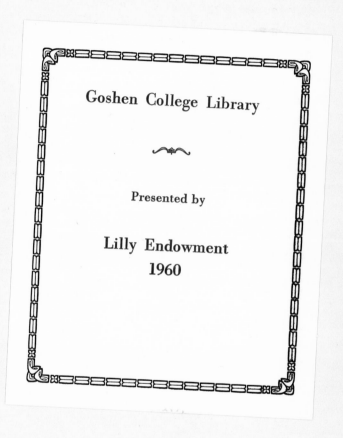

BRITAIN VIEWS OUR
INDUSTRIAL RELATIONS

Britain Views Our
INDUSTRIAL RELATIONS

MARK J. FITZGERALD, C.S.C.

Associate Professor of Economics
University of Notre Dame

UNIVERSITY OF NOTRE DAME PRESS

NOTRE DAME, INDIANA

ACKNOWLEDGMENTS

The inclination to take up the work which preceded the writing of this book is due in great part to J. Lawrence O'Toole who first called my attention to the reports of the Anglo-American productivity teams.

Raymond F. Cour, C.S.C., Louis F. Buckley, and Robert Johnston read the entire manuscript and made helpful suggestions. Nicholas M. Di Pietro has given me useful comments in regard to several portions of the work.

I am grateful to William M. Burke for his valuable literary criticism.

Particular thanks are due to Joseph R. Gambardella who typed each chapter.

Much of the research done in England was made possible through the courtesy of T. A. Prichard who provided introductions to union, management and government officials.

TABLE OF CONTENTS

BRITAIN VIEWS OUR INDUSTRIAL RELATIONS

CHAPTER ONE

Purpose of the British Visits to America

The last report has now been published in the series of 67 British union-management studies by teams which have visited industries in the United States since 1948. Under the sponsorship of the Anglo-American Council on Productivity these industrial reports were initiated in the belief that there are sufficient factors common to British and American industry to warrant a careful analysis of American experience. In several ways the team visits helped to foster a new form of international public relations. It is true that over the years representatives of British companies and unions have visited this country for the purpose of comparison and analysis. Yet nothing in the past approached the scope and systematic method characteristic of these recent industrial studies.

Facing the urgency of maintaining economic stability at home while confronted with severely competitive world markets and rising armament costs, both unions and management in the United Kingdom at the end of World War II agreed that greater productivity at lower per unit cost was the path to British recovery and a higher standard of living. Both employers and employees in Britain regarded it as futile to attempt to raise living standards by the simple expedient of general wage increases unsupported by corresponding improvement in productivity. Without the latter element it was felt that no enhancement in real wages would result. True a monetary rise in income might develop, but it could soon be cancelled by inflationary price changes.

Effort to expand industrial output merely by employing more manpower reached its limit in 1948. The substantial postwar increase in over-all production by that year of thirty percent above the 1938 level had been achieved largely through adding about two million more workers to the labor force than were employed before World War II. Further efforts in this direction were narrowly restricted to inducing workers in less important jobs to take employment in vital industries. The influx of 160,000 displaced persons from the Continent helped in only a limited degree toward stepping up British production an additional twenty percent so necessary to reach a balance in foreign trade. With full employment a reality it was obvious to responsible leaders in Britain that future efforts in the direction of expanded output would not be through the addition of substantially more workers, but rather by making each operative more productive.

ANGLO-AMERICAN COUNCIL

To aid in the achievement of greater industrial output the Anglo-American Council on Productivity was established in 1948 at the invitation of Sir Stafford Cripps, then Chancellor of the Exchequer and Mr. Paul G. Hoffman, at that time Administrator of the Economic Co-operation Administration.[1] Making up the Council were representatives of management and unions in both the United Kingdom and the United States. The thirteen British members of the Council were selected by the Federation of British Industries, the British Employers' Confederation, and the Trades Union Congress. The eight American members included corporation presidents, a former head of the National Association of Manufacturers, and representatives from unions in the A. F. of L., the C. I. O., and the Railroad Brotherhoods.[2] The Council had for its objective the best methods by which American and British industries might co-operate in furthering efforts to raise productivity in the United Kingdom. It was the conviction of the Council that by proper utilization of competent leadership in management and labor the talents and resources of the United Kingdom could be concentrated on expanding industrial output.[3] In addition a more progressive view on expanded use of capital equipment was expected to result from the influence and guidance of the Productivity Council. Moreover, hope was expressed that not only would British recovery be hastened by this approach, but also an improved economy on the Continent would follow as well.

PRODUCTIVITY TEAMS

Members of the Council realized that success in expanding industrial output rests on a diverse group of factors, each one requiring its proper degree of emphasis. To become familiar with some of the best practices in industrial know-how and techniques the Council decided in 1948 that a series of plant visits should be made to the

United States by productivity teams representing the various industries in the United Kingdom. Members of such teams were appointed jointly by trade associations, employer federations, and trade unions of particular industries. They represented proportionately managerial, technical, and operational levels and commonly numbered fifteen members.

PURPOSE

Primarily the British teams sought to determine the factors which accounted for the high rate of American industrial productivity. In this quest the team members endeavored to find the explanation for the markedly different attitudes of mind toward productivity which seem to prevail in America. Throughout the program each industrial team confined itself to the American counterpart of the industry it represented in Great Britain.

To insure a systematic approach some areas of inquiry common to all the team visits included technical processes, handling of materials, production control, types of plant and equipment, and industrial relations. The latter term of reference, industrial relations, is the particular phase of the team reports which forms the core of discussion in this volume. As a stimulus to action later, the teams wished to draw conclusions from their findings which might serve for recommendations to management, unions, and government in Britain.

SELECTION OF TEAMS

In determining the composition of the productivity teams care was taken to give full representation to the structural organization of British industry and thereby insure that proportionate weight would be given to the recommendations by the teams on their return to Britain. Accordingly trade unions as well as employer groups have been the organizations used in selecting candidates for team membership.[4]

Moreover, the representatives selected from these groups were required to have sufficiently wide experience or equivalent technical knowledge to make it likely that they would be discerning observers when studying their own industry in America. Selection was made from both large and small firms and over the widest possible geographical area. Decided advantage was gained from including a full time union official on each team whenever possible. His participation made it easier to discuss matters with American trade union officials and insured a wide consideration to the team's report in British trade union groups on the occasions of conferences and seminars.

Upon laying down these general requirements, the Anglo-American Council left the actual task of selection to the nominating committees jointly represented by employer and union groups in the various industries. Gratification has since been expressed by the Council with the high standard of participation which resulted from this method of drawing up the teams.[5]

The total membership of the 67 teams which visited the United States during the Council's program numbered over 900. They collectively made observations in almost 2,000 plants or enterprises in America. Special mention has been given by the Council of the willingness with which British firms and other organizations made available their key members to take part in these long and difficult assignments.[6]

Most of the major industries in Britain sent productivity teams to America under the program. Upon receiving a request from a British industry to make such a team journey, the Council would consult representatives of the same industry in America. When word was received that the visit would be welcomed, steps were taken to make up a team. Before seeking approval from America, the Council made certain that the industry requesting authorization for a productivity team was of sufficient importance in the British economy to warrant representation in the program.[7] Moreover, in presenting the request to the U. S. Section of the Council, the various branches of the industry to be represented were clearly described, together with the number and average size of the firms to be reflected in the team's membership. Data were also forwarded on the volume of production and the amount of exports credited to the industry in question.

Since a number of particular questions relating to productivity were of concern to a wide range of industries, it was decided to send to America a number of specialist teams which were to follow a somewhat different pattern of investigation than used by most of the teams. Yet, while the size and composition of each of the specialist groups were designed to meet the peculiar needs of the subject under study, no departure was made in the case of the specialist teams from the principle of maintaining representation from both unions and management. Of the 67 teams which came to America, 19 were in the specialist category. In determining their composition, the Council received co-operation from universities and professional institutions as well as from trade unions and employer associations.

FINANCES

At the outset the Anglo-American Council decided that all the costs incurred by the teams while on British soil, that is, sterling cost, would be paid for by the United Kingdom. In turn the Economic Cooperation Administration of the United States met the traveling and living expenses of the teams while they were in America.

As of 1952 the total expenses thus borne by the United Kingdom amounted to $897,000. The share assumed by the American government came to $1,467,000. Most of the British financing, $504,000, was covered by a grant from the British Treasury and by contributions from employer associations and the Trades Union Congress. An additional sum of $394,800 was contributed by the industries directly represented by the productivity teams.[8] Note should be taken of the generous contribution in time made by American industry and union officials to assure the success of the tours of investigation while the teams were in the United States. By the same token British companies and unions should be given credit for their generosity in permitting former team members to take out time from regular duties for lectures and panel meetings during a period of many months after formal completion of a team's program.

OPERATION OF THE TEAMS

To provide proper knowledge of an industry in Britain which was represented by a productivity team, the members made a series of visits to several plants in England before leaving for America. The Council stated that a background confined to one firm would not insure adequate knowledge of the various modes of operation in the industry throughout the British Isles. This preliminary briefing tour also gave an opportunity to try out in practice the procedure to be used while in the United States. For the British industry represented by the team, the preliminary tour likewise increased the attention given the productivity program by companies not directly participating through team membership.

On the point of departure for the United States each team attended a briefing session conducted by the British Section of the Council. Both at the start and at the completion of the tour through American plants additional briefing sessions for team members were held in New York by the United States Section of the Council. The initial briefing sessions were designed to recheck procedures and to make certain that the questionnaires for gathering information were sufficiently detailed and covered all the points of reference proper to the industry. At the concluding session after the tour, members were asked to comment on their experiences and to present any unresolved issues to Council officials or labor advisors.[9]

While a team was going about its series of plant visits, all the members were accorded similar treatment in the matter of meals, living accommodations, and dollar allowances. A sense of common purpose and understanding was a natural consequence of this democratic policy. Save for some cases of visits to small plants, it was found undesirable to divide a team into separate groups for independent itineraries. All levels of an industry from top management to shop workers were included in a plant visit since at each stage special insights might be obtained on the various aspects of productivity.

On an average a team toured three or four plants each

week. The total number of plants covered by the 67 teams approximated 2,000.[10]

Within a particular plant a visit usually began with a brief orientation meeting. A tour of the establishment would then follow in groups according to particular interests if enough guides were available. Care was taken to insure that adequate time was allowed for discussion between individuals or groups representing the same level of plant operation. Stress was placed on keeping a plant tour as informal and flexible as possible so that extra time for certain members might be given to matters of special concern to them.

PREPARING THE REPORTS

The representatives from management, unions, and technical divisions of British industry who participated in the team visits were well aware of the crucial importance of the report to be made on their work. Views expressed in such publications were the responsibility of the members themselves, and the Council avoided any action which might be construed as interference with the expression of a team's findings. Upon returning to England, the team leader and team secretary would reassemble the members periodically for a series of meetings while the report was being drafted. In some instances such meetings lasted for several days at a time.[11] Only in matters of arrangement of materials for greater uniformity and readability were the services of expert advisors from the Council utilized during this period. Because of many interruptions, inevitable after an absence from regular duties for about two months while traveling on team visits, final drafts of reports were seldom completed in less than four months. Characterized by a high degree of team participation, the reports can truly be regarded as the fruit of a joint effort. It is worthy of note that with one exception, the team findings were unanimous.

RELEASING OF THE REPORTS

Every effort was made to time the publication of a report with the scheduling of a special conference of the industry so that the teams' findings and recommendations could be discussed to best advantage. Special committees were appointed to consider particular divisions of a report. For example questions dealing with industrial relations were turned over to a joint session of the employers' federation and the trade union of a particular industry.[12]

To encourage the widest hearing for a team's account at time of publication, the Council aided in the distribution of copies throughout the industry concerned. Circulation of reports to employer federations and trade unions in other industries was sponsored by the kindred organizations represented on the productivity team.

A number of industries have followed the technique used when the Report on the Grey Ironfounding industry was published. In this instance a conference on the report was held by the industry's association and the printed proceedings of the question and answer sessions were later circulated over a wide area. In general the most practical approach was to conduct separate meetings of union and management groups when discussing team reports. Decided success, however, has also characterized joint meetings of union and management representatives. During the course of disseminating the findings in a productivity report, the number of meetings attended by employers, union officials and operatives have averaged 30 to 40 in the course of a year or more. In the case of meetings held by the Cotton Spinning team over 3,000 leading representatives of the industry attended a total of 40 meetings. Several employer organizations have held special conventions over a period of three or four days to discuss the productivity reports for their industries.[13]

As early as 1952 over 500,000 copies of team reports had been sold to research organizations and to the general public. Popular digests of the reports were circulated in even larger numbers than the original publications for the benefit of men and women on the shop floor.[14]

There is overwhelming evidence that the time willingly given by team members to the work of making known the findings and recommendations in the reports far exceeded the amount originally contemplated. Demand for the services of team representatives for lectures and panel discussions continued on almost a weekly basis even after two years following the publication of a report. The Council believes that the industrial and social contacts of the more than 900 men and women who made up the teams have served to develop a changed attitude on the importance of increased productivity over ever widening circles of union and management groups.[15]

Emphasis has been given by the Council to the crucial point that the real test of the success won by any team's report is the action taken at the plant level by both management and workers. Unless at this stage a report awakens a real understanding of the problem and a desire to raise levels of industrial output by improved methods of work, no contribution of lasting value will have been made. Present indications show that hoped for results are being realized. A steady repetition of the same themes in different industries is having a favorable effect toward widening the realization that the key to Britain's future prosperity lies in a higher rate of industrial output.[16]

CHAPTER TWO

Management Policy on Industrial Relations

Among the points in this area which are stressed in the present chapter is the increasing importance attached to departments of industrial relations in American companies and the care taken to maintain an active two-way communication channel between management and workers. Attention is given to the union-company scope of collective bargaining as compared with the British practice of industry-wide bargaining. Joint consultation between unions and management and the use of the grievance process are examined. Note is taken of the American approach to apprentice training and promotion. Comments from team reports are noted as they relate to unemployment pools and absenteeism. Impressions are also cited on American methods of utilizing manpower.

GROWING EMPHASIS ON INDUSTRIAL RELATIONS

In the estimation of the British team which studied the Munitions industry, American management places great importance on problems dealing with industrial relations. Members of the team were impressed by the fact that in both the union and non-union plants visited the department of industrial relations operated with a much larger staff of personnel than is customary in British industry. They attributed this greater size of the industrial relations unit to the high degree of autonomy accorded to such departments in America. Moreover, internal divisions of the industrial relations section are permitted to carry on specialized functions dealing with such matters as training of operatives, job classification and evaluation, advisory boards, and grievance committees.[1]

The British productivity team on Packet Foods which inspected 15 plants in this industry between New York and Minneapolis in 1951 agreed that American management generally devotes a considerable amount of attention to intelligent treatment of its employees. Yet it was observed that this general practice in America is duplicated at least by the best managements in Britain.[2] Members of the team representing the British Cakes and Biscuits industry, who in 1951 made a coast to coast tour of bakeries in the United States, concluded that in the past five years especially there has been considerable "hard thinking" given to the various phases of industrial relations by American companies. The effort had borne fruit in terms of well planned organization and methods in this field. It was noted that at times a vice-president is in charge of industrial relations, thus giving his department a top-ranking status.[3]

Quite the exception to the findings of most reports, members of the Machine Tools team gathered the impression that American companies in this industry generally do not look upon organized labor as an accepted institution. Particularly in the smaller plants, it was learned that management prefers to make agreements with its workers without the intervention of any union. In quite a number of plants this team found that no union contracts existed whatever.

Moreover, it was learned that companies which did not have a union contract endeavored to outmatch unionized plants in terms of better working conditions. Constant effort was made to remind the workers of these superior conditions in anticipation of a possible election on the union or non-union issue.[4]

COMMUNICATION

Members of the team covering the Internal Combustion Engine industry noted in their report that in the larger plants, it was the policy to post bulletins and news items for all employees on developments in company policy. As a result most workers after twelve months of service are in a position to discuss factory matters in an intelligent fashion. By the realization that he was being provided with all possible information and was told the reasons for changes in organization, the average worker in the large corporations took pride in his company and its products. Reasons were given for changes in such matters as plant layout, arrangement of staff, and general policy. The British team members believed this practice helped to stop at the source critical comments often stemming from absence of information.[5]

Another aspect of industrial relations noted by the members of the Internal Combustion Engine team was the large number of operatives known personally by senior executives even in the larger plants. The team members attributed this situation to the fact that many administrative officers had themselves been once employed on the workshop floor.[6] Concerning this same point, the report of the productivity team on Pharmaceuticals, written after a tour of seventeen drug firms in the United States during the late fall of 1950, stated that there is no question that less plant formality exists among all grades of individuals in America than is the case in Britain.[7] Many productivity teams, including Pharmaceuticals, commented on the American custom of using first names when workers and management representatives address each other on the job. The members of the Brassfoundry industry stated that while this apparent friendliness may not necessarily be indicative of good relations, it does express an attitude of sincerity between management and workers as well as their realization of mutual dependence.[8]

Nevertheless, a considerable number of team members who covered the Machine Tools industry formed the impression that even though American workers address a foreman, manager, or even a vice-president in a plant by his first name, it does not necessarily indicate a more cordial attitude than is found in British plants. The British visitors regarded the familiarity as merely a habit of long standing, without particular significance.[9]

The British team covering the Valve industry noted that the efficient staff organization in American plants freed management from pressure of details. This freedom was often used by management to move about the plant frequently, thus becoming able to know many operatives personally. One case was cited where the president of a company knew personally almost one-half of the 1,500 employees in his work force.[10]

Members of the Brassfoundry team stated that the very term workman had a different connotation in America than in Britain. No rigid class customs bound the American worker in regard to what recreation or amenities he should seek. They found the feeling general that a worker, the same as anyone else, had the right to whatever betterment in life he could earn by his own efforts. Moreover, team members rarely could recognize an American workman as such outside the plant. Unlike in Britain, these men often come to work well dressed and in their own cars. Convenient changing rooms, found in plants of all sizes, contain lockers for operatives so they can dress for the street or for work. In effect the report on the Brassfoundry industry concluded that there is not as sharp a line of division between worker and employer in this industry as is the case in Britain. American employees earn sizable incomes, to English observers, and can afford to own cars and indulge in diversions beyond the hope of most British workers.[11]

COLLECTIVE BARGAINING

Though the team covering Cotton Spinning found an industry-wide employers' association in operation, the American Cotton Manufacturer's Institute, the team learned that this association did not take part in industrial relations. Such matters were negotiated by individual employers and their workers. Even so, it was found that the local branches of the national association tended to discuss among themselves wages and working conditions on either a formal or an informal basis. An instance was noted where the Textile Workers' Union, C. I. O., signed joint contracts with the local Textile Manufacturers' Association in Fall River and New Bedford, regulating wages and working conditions in all the mills under the control of the signers.[12]

The British Furniture team saw nothing in the United States comparable to the British National Labour Agreement for the Furniture Manufacturing Trade which establishes basic terms for the entire industry. Nor did this team encounter an organization similar to the British Furniture Trade Joint Industrial Council, representing organized labor and management, which permits mutual discussion on matters of common concern.[13]

In passing judgment on the merit of restricting collective bargaining to one company or even one plant, a number of the British productivity reports had grounds for criticism. The team covering Steel Foundries believed that while separate contracts between companies and the Steelworkers' Union might foster a competitive spirit, it appeared that disharmony between companies and the union was thus encouraged, especially at the time when contracts are being renegotiated. The members of this team saw nothing in such an arrangement that would encourage more productivity.[14] The report on the Pressed Metal industry considered that restriction of collective bargaining to a union-company basis made it possible for the unions to pit one employer against another as a point of strategy. Fear was expressed that serious harm might result to certain employers and ultimately perhaps to workers themselves.[15] The members of the Non-Ferrous Metals team believed that the present British organizational structure of unions would make impossible the adaptation of union-company collective bargaining.[16]

The productivity team covering the Food Canning industry expressed agreement with the report of the Internal Combustion Engine team that negotiation on the local level absorbed an excessive amount of time of union officials. It was also believed that this method of negotiation necessitated high union fees to defray expenditures. The costly duplication of effort was regarded as inferior to the British method of negotiation on a national scale.[17]

JOINT CONSULTATION

Within the area of negotiation itself, the British productivity teams sought to determine just how much formal joint consultation existed between union and management on a permanent basis. Members of the team representing the Brush industry considered that this type of co-operation is essential for the attainment of maximum production.

Yet a number of the British teams were surprised to learn of the relatively slight development of joint consultation among the various industries in America. The team covering the Pharmaceutical industry stated that it encountered no joint bodies of unions and management similar to the joint advisory committees or the works councils common in British industry. Instead of an industry-wide forum for the open discussion of mutual difficulties, the handling of these issues is usually limited to the plant-local union area within the restrictions of the contract.[18]

The special report on *Trade Unions and Productivity* by British Trade Union Officials under the sponsorship of the Trades Union Congress also expressed surprise at the lack of interest shown by many American union leaders in the use of formal machinery for joint consultation, even though many unions in the United States have the resources to make notable contributions to greater plant efficiency. As an explanation of this situation the British Trade Union Officials surmised that most American unions neither expect nor desire to be consulted by management about the operation of the plant. Many American unions prefer to let management take the initiative, within the terms of the contract, and then decide on proper union action after the event. The British Trade Unions' team found a more receptive attitude, however, toward joint consultation on the part of unions possessing alert technical departments and operating in industries where management suffered from backwardness and inefficiency.[19]

The team which inspected plants in the Cotton Yarn Doubling industry saw no indication of any method used similar to the works councils in Britain for joint consultation on matters relating to management policy and practice. It is the belief of American company officials in the Cotton Yarn Doubling industry that the daily contact between workers and supervisory staff suffices. In some plants, however, provision is also made for consideration of suggestions from employees.[20]

The report on the Food Canning industry noted that while during the last war joint works councils had been set up in many plants, they had pretty well been discarded by 1951 and with the approval of the trade unions. It was learned that the unions consider the existence of such joint councils as a restrictive influence on the prestige and authority of union officials. Of the eighteen food canning plants visited, in only one factory was the works council from the last war still in operation.[21]

The productivity team representing the British Cakes and Biscuit industry found that much attention was given in America to informal, daily consultation. Particular note was made of the foreman-shop steward arrangement in the American factory.[22] If an issue warrants more consideration, discussion is carried on with union representatives at a higher level. Most teams, however, found little indication of joint committees similar to those in Britain, made up of management-appointed and worker-elected delegates meeting regularly for joint consultation before certain managerial decisions take final form.

A rather exceptional case to this general picture was noted in the team report on the Footwear industry. Unlike the usual relation which seemed to prevail between unions and companies in the Shoe industry, the team found that at least one company and an independent union, the Industrial Union of Master Craftsmen, acknowledged an equal voice to the other on certain managerial decisions. In effect the union and the company by equal authority set the wage brackets and ultimate earnings possible for the operatives. Moreover, the union maintained time study experts who were accepted on an equal basis with the consultants retained by the company. Full information on the profit and loss position of the company was regularly provided the business agent who had an office on the premises of the company. Approval by the union business office was required before any operatives could be hired or fired. It was noted in the Footwear report that the company in this case has been able to operate at full employment for more than twenty years and has been free of troubled labor relations.[23]

The members of the team covering Meat Packaging and Processing encountered no formal methods for joint consultation of the type prevailing in Britain. They stated that means of communication between management and workers usually depended on the intermittent flow of information to the shop floor through the regular management and supervisory channels. Judging from the language of typical union-management contracts in the Packing industry, the British team came to the conclusion that workers accepted the policy that operational decisions should be left to management. This same team learned that experiments in the past with joint consultation similar to the English pattern had been attempted, but without success.[24]

The special team of British Trade Union Officials found a good illustration of joint consultation existing between an electrical manufacturing company in Detroit and the International Brotherhood of Electrical Workers. In this instance a joint production committee, composed of three appointed union representatives and three management representatives, meets every week to discuss problems relating to production. The British Union Officials were impressed by the fact that the local union president, a paid employee of the company, is allowed to devote his full time to handling union matters within the plant. His attention is given to checking on participation in time studies, handling grievances, and obtaining, when necessary, counsel from the international union.[25] The team of British Union Officials noted that many other American companies also retain union representatives or shop stewards on a full time basis to handle production matters relating to the union.

Despite the absence of formal joint consultation in most of the plants visited the British Trade Union Officials believed that union-management relations in America are generally better than in many British plants. Moreover, they stated that union-company agreements in the United

States to a great extent cover matters which are left to joint consultative committees in the United Kingdom.

The British Union Officials found that typical union contracts in America give detailed attention to dispute and grievance procedure. The local union is usually able to deal immediately with problems which arise and thus the infrequent need for outside consultation is mostly confined to very critical matters. The great stress in America on plant level bargaining has enabled the union local to settle most problems on wage rates without turning to the national union. In effect the British Union Officials found the local in America thoroughly responsive to company policy and aware that the economic stability of both the company and the union local depend on high productive efficiency. The report of the British Union Officials, however, observed that while employers in America accommodate themselves to strong unions which are established in the plants, little heed is paid to weak labor organizations which have not won bargaining rights by majority representation.[26]

The report of the team covering the Electricity Supply industry stated that some forms of consultation by management, supervisors, and employees existed in varying degree in all the public utilities visited. In certain instances group decisions were worked out by consultation between supervisors and the groups responsible to them. It was noted that the top management realized the worth of participation by both supervisors and operatives in the shaping of plans and the methods to implement them. Management officials stated that a decision shared in by employees is a decision employees will endeavor to support.

Actual use of regular committees in regard to joint consultation is found chiefly on matters of safety programs. The Electricity Supply team encountered such committees in most of the plants visited and on a departmental basis. In one case a large public utility company maintained regularly scheduled joint committee meetings in its departments and discussed such matters as efficiency, and methods of bettering the performance of the departments. Wages and working conditions, however, were not considered.[27]

The Electricity Supply team was impressed with the system of joint co-operative committees and conferences in operation under the Tennessee Valley Authority. These groups cover employees within the scope of the Trades and Labor Council and the Salary Policy Employee Panel for the Tennessee Valley. While the policy for employee relationship was a unilateral creation of the T. V. A. management in 1935, the Electricity Supply team pointed out in its report that preceding it was joint study and the basic agreement by the employees as expressed by the representatives of their unions. The official statement of the T. V. A. on joint consultation directs that joint discussion might dwell on such matters as prevention of waste in construction and production, improvement in quality of worker performance, correction of conditions leading to grievances, promotion of safety, and better working conditions.

The Electricity Supply Report noted that joint committees and conferences are established on a local basis both at construction jobs and in operating establishments of the T. V. A. These local committees and conferences are given basic guidance and overall co-ordination by a joint co-operative unit. The objective pointed out for these local organizations is the development of a co-operative spirit which will lead to greater efficiency in performance.

The Electricity Supply team learned that management in T. V. A. sets great store by the volume of suggestions received from members of local joint committees and conferences, regarding them as the best indication of actual participation by employees in union-agreement consultation. A two-way benefit was noted by T. V. A. officials in the use of these committees and conferences. They promoted better methods of operation and a psychological lift for the employees in knowing that management appreciates their contributions toward the improvement of efficiency. To insure steady development of such committees the Electricity Supply team found that training courses for managers and supervisors included special sessions on the methods and techniques of joint consultation and decision. An efficient information service supplemented these training courses.[28]

In regard to the impact of joint consultation on management, members of the team representing the Cotton Spinning industry stated that existing relations between management and workers in the plants visited gave no indication that management was losing its prerogatives. This observation was applied to both union and non-union companies. Moreover, the Cotton Spinning Report indicated that where management made known to workers the reasons for important orders, particularly those affecting working conditions, a better response was obtained from the operatives.[29]

The productivity team on Coal Mining found that the attitude of the United Mine Workers showed acceptance of the belief that the actual conduct of operations should be left to management. Unlike some of the other industries visited by the British teams, the United Mine Workers showed little interest in joint consultation. The British Coal team gathered that the American Mine Workers sought no share in company decisions nor any advance notice of company intentions. Survival of the mining companies was their own affair and if inefficient managements failed, the Coal industry as a whole was the better for it.[30]

GRIEVANCE PROCEDURE

The productivity team representing the British Pressed Metal industry was much impressed with the phase of joint consultation in America which dealt with the handling of grievances. The members of this team noted that the grievance committee in each plant, made up of representatives from management and workers, met regularly once or twice a month. Approval was expressed for the definite time period assigned to each stage of the grievance procedure and to the practice of requesting the aggrieved party to put his complaint in writing over his signature. These two features were considered by the British team to be a powerful influence in lessening discontent and in fostering co-operative relationships.

The report on the Pressed Metal industry stated that if American grievance procedure were adopted in Britain, a serious cause of industrial unrest would be removed since the belief that a grievance is being tardily handled often causes more trouble than the original complaint.[31] The team covering the Cotton Yarn Doubling industry found that even in unionized mills there is no objection to personal presentation of grievances to management by the workers directly as long as the final adjustment does not conflict with the wage structure in the plant and a union representative may be present during the procedure.[32]

While emphasizing that in problems of employer-employee relations American workers do not appear either more or less amenable or intelligent than British operatives, the members of the Diesel Locomotives team declared that grievances are usually dispatched more expeditiously in America. In accounting for their more facile solution in the States the team members attributed it to a "willingness-to-try-anything-once" and to the sense of urgency which characterizes the American scene.[33]

In the union agreement a formal method of approach is laid down for grievance procedure. In one mill it was found that the regular grievance committee of union and management representatives meets weekly to adjust cases. Mention was made of certain Southern mills, evidently non-union, where the "open door" policy is in force. In such mills the operative, in accordance with the employee hand book, may initiate his complaint with the overseer, and if not satisfied with the action taken, may seek redress by regular stages as high up as the vice-president of the company. No mention was made about the frequency with which employees take this final recourse.[34]

Calling attention to the similarity between British joint consultation and American grievance procedure, the report of the Internal Combustion Engines team observed that in its estimation grievance committees in America tend to deal with union affairs in general. At least in certain plants visited, the area involved a scope somewhat wider in range than indicated by the title, grievance procedure, attached to it.[35]

As an explanation for the more rapid adjustment of

grievances in America, the British productivity team which covered the American Iron and Steel industry noted that standardization of wages and working conditions greatly reduces the number of complaints among the many grades of employees within a plant and for the industry as a whole.[36] A somewhat different evaluation of American grievance procedure was contained in the report on the Electricity Supply industry. This team report noted that a framework comparable to the British Electricity Supply industry was lacking in most public utilities visited in the United States. The existing methods for settling grievances in the American electric power industry were considered at most no better than the regular British practice in the same industry.[37]

APPRENTICE TRAINING

Reporting on the problem of apprenticeship training in America, the Building team noted that at the end of World War II this industry in the United States found itself severely undermanned. Severe reduction in the rate of immigration since the 1930's and long standing restrictions on entrance into the Building trade unions were regarded as important causes of the shortage. One result was the high age level of many craftsmen. For instance bricklayers averaged 55, and carpenters, 58 years respectively.

To meet the problem, the Building trades, aided by the Federal government, instituted apprenticeship training courses throughout the country with a broader and more regular basis than previously regarded as necessary. Spurred on by the emergency, both unions and management co-operated to improve the standards of the Building crafts.

The role of both the Federal and state governments in this training program was largely confined to consultation and exhortation, leaving the main responsibility for the actual training to the Building industry itself. Accordingly the authority to select applicants and to organize and supervise their apprenticeships was vested in more than 3,000 Joint Apprenticeship Committees over the nation. These groups endeavored to estimate future labor needs and to provide the programs in school and on the job for the trainees.

Relaxation of age requirements was permitted in the case of the returning war veterans. Moreover, the industry adopted a ruling which permitted veterans who passed certain trade tests during their apprenticeship to shorten their training period and thus qualify earlier for the regular craft wage rates. The Building team contrasted the veterans' program in the United States, administered and controlled by industry, with the corresponding British program which was government controlled. One advantage seen in the American course of training was that it made assimilation into industry easier for the American veterans. No prejudice on the part of employers or workers was felt toward ex-soldiers on the grounds that the government was turning them over to the Building industry only partially trained and at wage rates not warranted by their abilities.

Members of the Building team considered that inclusion of veterans under the regular apprenticeship training program was made all the easier because the average age for entrance into the trades in America is much higher than in Britain. It was found that most youths in America entering the Building crafts had pursued a course of general education until 17 or 18 years of age. In contrast, British boys usually become apprentices at 15 or 16. Further, the top age for acceptance in the United States, age 25, is much above the British level; and the period of training is often shorter in the States, averaging from three to five years.

Another advantage seen in the regulations for American apprenticeship was that the maturer age of the applicants reduced greatly the wastage during the training period since the candidates were more surely set on their choice of a career. Again, a more intensive training is possible since the applicant enters the program at a higher stage of mental, educational, and physical development.

To prevent any problems of assimilation, an American youth may not become an apprentice in certain trades unless he has first obtained a union card and an offer of employment from a builder. Meeting these requirements, he then enters into an agreement with the Joint Apprenticeship Committee related to his particular craft. Unlike in Britain, the apprentice receives no indenture assuring continuous employment with a particular firm. As a result the employer is free to discharge the apprentice at any time. It would then fall upon the Joint Committee to find employment for him with some other firm.

In regard to standards, the Joint Committee establishes the technical curriculum for the training period so that the national minimum standard will be attained. Periodically trade tests are given to the apprentice, and trainees deficient in some areas of apprenticeship are warned they will be dropped if two successive tests are failed.[38]

A generally favorable effect of the American apprentice system was noted by the report of the Welding team. This group concluded that the American employee has a broader outlook and is more receptive to adapting himself in his adult life to specialized jobs on the basis of a short-term period of training. Moreover, the Welding team learned that the dismissed employee in America has a greater opportunity for finding alternative work in some other industry than is the case in Britain. Transfer of skills in America apparently faces by no means the severe obstacles prevalent in Britain. Accordingly, the members of this team felt that American workers are less prone to fear the consequences of running out of work in a particular craft.[39]

Speaking of typical American machine operators or engine assemblers, the British team covering the Internal Combustion Engine industry observed that such operatives enter employment completely unskilled. With the training given them by the foreman, however, they are able in a few weeks to set up their own work and earn a bonus. Extreme simplification of assembly operations and machining has made this achievement possible. More complicated tasks, such as a turret lathe operation, can be mastered over a period of a few months by training under the supervision of a foreman.

The team members were so impressed by this rapid development of skills in America that they were inclined to ask whether the present British apprentice system is in need of overhauling and even replacement by a more concentrated program. They noted that the basis for such a revision is strengthened by the restricted skill presently required of operatives and by the greater mechanical aptitude now characteristic of boys when leaving school. The Internal Combustion Engine team observed that where more extensive skill is required in American plants, for instance in electrical and maintenance departments, traditional apprenticeship periods are still in effect.[40]

UPGRADING

Members of the Lithographic team noted in their report the readiness with which unskilled workers in America are permitted to upgrade themselves by completing a course of apprenticeship. The team believed this circumstance may help to explain the obvious lack of social distinction between skilled and unskilled workers in the Lithographic industry.[41] This attitude of American workers contrasts sharply with the situation in Great Britain.

Union officials and operatives in the United States regard even college trained personnel favorably since they bring a specialized type of background which improves the general efficiency of the plant. However, the British team visiting the Cotton Weaving industry discovered that Northern mills were experiencing a handicap from a shortage of the right type of worker who might advance to executive positions. As a result one company now provides college scholarships both for younger employees and for children of employees. It is the policy of this firm to fill managerial vacancies with employees who have obtained degrees by means of these scholarships, providing that evidence of ability and leadership is demonstrated beforehand.[42]

According to the Grey Ironfounding team a great number of university graduates enter industrial workshops and foundries rather than the usual laboratories and offices. The members of this team believed that the presence of so many young men in American industrial plants with thorough technical training and receptive minds helps to account for the versatility and vigor of American industry.[43]

FOREMEN

In the opinion of the British union-management team studying the American Munitions industry, a greater percentage of foremen in this country have come from the shop floor. The team members found that in most instances the foreman did not exercise the power to discharge employees. According to the usual procedure he makes a recommendation for discharge to the director of industrial relations. In any event the Munitions team believed that on matters of promotion and discharge far more weight is given to the views and recommendations of the foremen in America than is customary in the United Kingdom.[44]

UNEMPLOYMENT POOLS

Members of the British team which studied the Building industry in America maintained that a factor which helps to account for high speed and quality of performance among workers on many record-breaking building projects in America is the constant awareness of the pool of unemployed associated with the Building industry. Knowledge that another man can readily be found to take his place was regarded as a strong incentive for the average worker to keep up a high standard of output. This British team observed, moreover, that the transition to the ranks of the unemployed in America brings about a sharper drop in the standard of living in America than in Britain since there is a larger variance between average earnings and unemployment benefits in America. Again, the effects of unemployment can be more drastic because the jobless

worker may lose much if not all of his household furnish-
ings. Purchase of such objects by time payments is now
widespread in the States.[45]

In complete disagreement with the importance given
above to the unemployment pool, the Brassfoundry team
declared that so far as workers in America are concerned
there is no foundation to the belief that an unemployment
pool is necessary to bring output to high levels. Instead
members of this team placed emphasis on the inherent
urge of the American to satisfy his own preference to
produce.[46]

A surprising contrast between present employment in
the British Shoe industry and the situation existing in the
Brockton area in Massachusetts was made by the team
studying this industry. It was the finding of the Footwear
team that under present circumstances only about eight
months' work each year was available in Brockton. While
it is true that between the two World Wars under-employ-
ment and unemployment existed in England, the situation
now is one of full-time employment for the average British
worker.[47]

The British productivity team which examined Freight
Handling in America called attention to another pool of
unemployment relating to the stevedores and longshoremen in New York City. It was found by the team members
that in general the casual worker is typical in this type of
freight handling. While it is true that men commonly
follow the work of a given employer, this fact of itself does
not assure steady employment. Especially in the longshor-
ing aspect of port activities the British visitors found a
great amount of labor in relation to the work available.
According to their finding, the Port of New York is able to
provide daily employment for only 60 percent of the num-

ber of men on hand. At the time of the team's visit in 1950 there was no registration plan in operation similar to that of the dock industry of Britain.[48]

ABSENTEEISM

In the estimation of the team which investigated the Coal Mining industry there was a noticeable difference in the rate of absenteeism between mechanized mines and those still using hand loading methods. Mines visited of the mechanized type had a record of voluntary absenteeism between 2 and 5 percent. In the nonmechanized mines, where records were obtained, the average rate of absenteeism for 1949 was 10 percent and in one month reached 17 percent. The samples taken, however, were far too few to be representative of all the 9,000 mines in the United States and thus no generalization could be made.

Nevertheless, the report of the Coal Mining team was inclined to credit American workers with a better record of attendance than their British counterparts. Several reasons were suggested to help explain this difference. As already implied, the first factor given credit is the great reduction in physical strain by working with mechanized equipment. Another important influence mentioned is the small working crew and its sharp reaction to persistent absences by any member of the unit. Neither the crew nor the Union, after fair warning, is inclined to show much sympathy to habitual offenders. Another point is the uncertainty throughout a large area of the Coal Mining industry in regard to the number of days in the year when work is to be available. Even in the years of war production, 1939–1948, the national average was 231 days, an exceptionally high range. By 1950 the figure had slumped to 171 days. As a consequence anxiety to meet living expenses keeps absenteeism in the Coal industry at a low percentage.

The members of the Coal Mining team also learned from American management that the installment plan for purchases likewise acts as a steadying force to keep miners on the job. Vast distances and hot summers, respectively, make the car and the refrigerator common necessities in many sections of America. Yet the average miner is unable to possess them except on the installment basis. To insure their retention in the home it is believed that the miner's wife plays an important role in keeping down the rate of absenteeism. Her anxiety, moreover, to solve the problem of paying for daily necessities over twelve months despite a short work year is another reason why she is given a large measure of credit for the steady work of her husband.

It is a policy amongst the larger coal firms systematically to check on absenteeism of more than two days in duration. If the cause lies in some domestic difficulty, help is forthcoming to meet it. Nevertheless, a prolonged absence with insufficient reason results in dismissal and replacement.[49]

Throughout American industry generally, the productivity team for the Iron and Steel industry concluded that labor turnover is higher than in the United Kingdom. No exception to this observation was found in the Steel industry. Of seven steel plants visited in the United States, with total employment of 75,000 workers, the annual turnover rate amounted to 24 percent. By way of contrast 24 heavy steel plants in Britain employing 87,500 workers had a turnover rate of only 15 percent in 1950.[50]

UTILIZATION OF MANPOWER

The productivity report of the team representing the Internal Combustion Engine industry, which visited the United States in the fall of 1949, found that an outstanding feature of American machine shops is the extent to which one man has the responsibility for the operation of several machines. The representatives from this British industry regarded such a situation to be a notable factor behind high levels of production in America. In one plant they saw six machines in the gear hobbing section controlled by one man. Another worker, besides caring for two automatic machines processing flywheels, also operated a multi-spindled drill, a tapping machine, and a manually controlled marking fixture.[51] Members of this team visited fifteen companies in the Internal Combustion Engine industry in such cities as Milwaukee, Detroit, Waukesha, and Melrose Park. A general observation made in the report of another productivity team also applies here. The comment was that upon entering an American factory the visitor from Britain is amazed at the relatively small number of operatives necessary to run the establishment.

The group representing the British Building industry, which in the summer of 1949 inspected building activities in such cities as New York, Chicago, Cleveland, Buffalo, and Boston, was impressed by the great speed with which American construction jobs were completed. Moreover, they considered the construction cost low as compared with the average rates of wages in the industry. Several factors were listed in the report of this team as having important bearing on the high productivity of the American

Construction industry. It was pointed out that projects are fully pre-planned and smooth co-ordination is maintained between subcontractors and the general contractor.

The British observers, however, declared that the new entrants to the industry in the United States are of a higher age group because of the longer attendance required in school. The consequent greater degree of maturity of the work force facilitates early attainment of proficiency.[52]

Members of the Cotton Yarn Doubling team pointed out in their report that over-all production is on a larger scale in this industry because of the abundance of trained textile workers in all regions. No machines stand idle for lack of experienced operatives to man them. Even a temporary absence from the job can be met by a transfer from some other occupation. In effect this circumstance permits a higher machine utilization in the American textile industry than in Britain.[53]

SUMMARY

The British teams were impressed by the high degree of autonomy permitted departments of industrial relations in American companies. Efforts to explain company policy to workers and the greater informality between management and men contrasted sharply with British practice. Little enthusiasm was shown for collective bargaining on the company level as compared with industry-wide bargaining in Britain. Joint consultation between unions and management was rarely encountered in the United States though it is widespread in Britain. Expeditious handling of grievances on definite time schedules set up in the union contract was commented on by many team members. Avoidance of rigid rules for apprentice training and the prevalence of more mature and longer schooled candidates were factors which the British teams held important in explaining why skills are developed rapidly in America. Pools of unemployment at peak prosperity were found in the Building industry, one sector of the Shoe industry, and among longshoremen. Of the several factors which tended to lessen absenteeism were listed the mechanization of work processes, pressure of installment payments, influence of wives, and resentment from fellow workers. Surprise was expressed at the relatively few workers necessary to operate machines in American factories as compared with the situation in Britain.

CHAPTER THREE

The Role of Unions in
American Industry

In this chapter impressions are noted on the attitude of American unions toward laborsaving devices. Comments from the reports refer here to the typical provisions found in union-management contracts, to the status of the union business agent, the shop steward and the union local. A mixed response to the American practice of union seniority is recorded. British findings are given on the development of research departments in a number of American unions. Observations by the teams are presented on the flexibility of modern union structure in this country and the attitude of American unions toward management. Remarks from the reports are cited on the role of unions here in regard to job evaluation, co-operation with management, and government regulation of industry.

LABORSAVING DEVICES

A firmly imbedded notion on the part of many people in America is the belief that unions generally adhere to a restrictive and obstructionist policy in regard to new methods of production. Without question instances of such practices can be found in a number of American unions. Yet, the pointed investigation by scores of British productivity teams throughout hundreds of plants in over fifty American industries indicates that American unions are fully aware that their own future prosperity depends upon improved standards of output and efficiency.

Members of the Cotton Spinning team, who visited cotton mills in Massachusetts and the Carolinas in the fall of 1949, found that the attainment of high productivity was a goal desired both by individual operators and by the unions representing them, the United Textile Workers, A. F. of L., and the Textile Workers Union, C. I. O.[1] The British specialist team on Welding, which visited over twenty American companies in the fall of 1950, observed that the number of employees had been reduced by promoting the best possible use of machines and by the advantage of an unimpeded flow of materials. This situation, it is to be noted, was not resented by the union organizations representing the employees and actually illustrated the joint desire of management and workers to obtain economical production. The team members pointed out that the unions representing welders emphasized that their agents and officers will aid in every possible manner to promote the highest degree of output and efficiency on the part of the union workers. Indeed, it was the concensus of the team members that unions in this field, as well as management, are "productivity conscious." [2]

A special team, mainly of engineers, from several British industries visited 21 factories in the United States to study methods of Materials Handling in industry. After discussing the subject with engineers, managers, workers, and union representatives, the team members came to the conclusion that workers and their unions offered no serious opposition to the introduction of new methods. It was found that management usually informed the union in advance of a change to permit opportunity for comment. Actually workers themselves often placed in the suggestion boxes proposals for greater use of mechanization. The report by this team stated that in the United States a man who is freed from manual work by a mechanical device often gets another job in the same plant or elsewhere, and perhaps as a machine operator.[3]

The team members representing the Grey Ironfoundry industry, who visited 24 grey iron foundries between New York and Chicago in the early months of 1950, learned that the majority union in this industry, the Molders and Foundry Workers Union, A. F. of L., believes that management should constantly strive to provide better facilities for a greater output. Moreover, representatives of this union stated that their organization stood ready to co-operate with management in repricing jobs, should disagreements arise when new methods necessitate a change in work flow. Further, the union endeavored to find new employment for displaced operatives. In effect, the union representatives made it clear that their organization did not blindly hold to a narrow policy of job protection and work restriction.[4]

Members of the productivity team representing the British Cotton Spinning industry, who in 1949 visited 12 cotton mills both in New England and in the South, stated that workers are disposed to give new devices and methods a fair trial based on a reasonable work assignment. The team members pointed out that the unions in this industry encourage the operatives in this attitude.[5] The members of this British team found that the unions in the Cotton Spinning industry regarded it as a special obligation on their part not only to persuade their own members but also to induce management as well to utilize every measure which will enhance productivity. To advance this objective, the union has trained some of its own men in work-study methods so they can offer constructive suggestions when work duties are being modified or are subject to negotiation.[6]

Members of the British special productivity team of Trade Union Officials noted in their report that an important contribution to greater output by American unions was their practice of spurring less efficient managements to adopt methods first sponsored by the leading companies. For the most part unions do not feel that it is necessary for them to devise new and better ways of production. Since a large sector of American management is constantly pioneering in this regard, the unions prefer to take a supporting role by widening the industrial area in which the new methods are adopted. As a consequence to their efforts towards raising the average efficiency of industry, the unions can look to greater average wage rates for their members.[7] Further, by informing less progressive managements of the technical know-how obtained through negotiations with more efficient companies, unions have found that the results are more effective than where the less efficient companies depend only on their technical associations and trade journals for knowledge of new developments.[8]

Expressing a somewhat different view, members of the British team which visited companies in the Valve industry in the United States noted that a number of union locals in that industry were not actively interested in the question of productivity. Their main concern seemed to be wage rates and working conditions as they related to individual plants. The British observers conjectured, however, that there was little need for union concern with productivity here since the present high standard of output was steadily improving. Moreover, it was found that the Valve unions showed no resentment toward management for initiating better methods or installing more efficient machinery, even when the change reduced the work force required for a given job.[9]

As a means of explaining the remarkably receptive attitude on the part of American unions to more efficient methods of production, the report of the specialist team on Welding observes that unions here are fully aware that strict economy of manpower is essential to insure the maintenance of a high standard of living. Since wage levels are high, unions generally are not surprised or resentful when management seeks to obtain more effective results with a reduced work force.[10] Members of the Cotton Yarn Doubling team, who visited 15 textile mills in Massachusetts, the Carolinas, Alabama, and Virginia during the fall of 1949, were impressed by the willingness with which management, unions, and operatives approached experimentation with new methods, and agreed to changes in work loads when the new methods disproportionately increased or decreased effort on the part of the employees.[11]

A similar finding was made by the team representing the British Rayon Weaving industry. This team which visited 22 American rayon plants in the East and South during the spring of 1949, stated in their report that there was evidence of a genuine readiness on the part of employees in the United States to adopt new methods of work which would lead to greater output. They were told by a prominent trade union official that in his view unions had no prerogative justifying them to make the decision whether or not more efficient machinery should be installed. Instead he believed unions should encourage their members to support every move to introduce new machinery which would accrue to the benefit of operatives.[12]

While unions in the Welding trade do not hesitate to challenge management when the speed of operations seems to be causing undue fatigue, members of the British Welding team saw no evidence that unions were usurping the function of management in regard to determining the general supervision and speed of operations. For instance, in the plants covered, no effort was made by the unions to restrict the number of machines of similar type which one man may operate.[13]

The special report by British Trade Union Officials did not overlook the fact that American unions differ in respect to the speed with which they believe technological changes should advance. Their report noted that while some unions in the United States regard retention of existent volume of employment as prior to all other considerations, the predominant attitude of American unions favors the continued introduction of new machinery and laborsaving devices. This situation seemed to indicate to the British observers that leaders of American unions were keenly aware of the economic advantage in a dynamic industrial structure.[14]

The team members pointed out that the new industrial unions, with little or no record of depression unemployment, are present in large numbers in American manufacturing. For many years these unions have seen surplus operatives, after the installation of laborsaving machinery, quickly reabsorbed in some other part of the same plant or industry. These new industrial unions believe that the very maintenance of their large memberships depends on dynamic technological changes which in turn develop new production and new demands.[15]

A deep-seated fear which has prompted some British unions to be hesitant in accepting laborsaving devices is this possibility of unemployment for their members, a situation the British call redundancy. By contrast, members of the team representing the British Brush industry, which covered 17 factories in the United States during the fall of 1950, noted that both American workers and union officials took pride in the high rates of output; and while doing so gave little heed to possible redundancy of workers or excessive production.[16] In the American Textile unions during 1949 the attitude seemed to prevail that whatever dislocation of workers may result from more mechanization will be only of a temporary nature. Members of the Cotton Yarn Doubling team found that textile workers were accustomed to see mechanization increase the total number of jobs and provide higher standards of living and less fatiguing conditions of work.[17]

One of the strongest pressure groups in the Coal industry for greater mechanization has been the United Mine Workers' Union. Moreover, the large amount of redundancy which has resulted has been viewed calmly both by union members and by union officials. Members of the productivity team on Coal Mining were told by union officials that mechanization permits the reduced work force to enjoy higher wages, reduced hours, and better working conditions. For those who are displaced more and cheaper coal will help to provide new jobs in other industries. The team members found that coal miners tended to share the general belief that the American economy is capable of absorbing workers displaced by mechanization. The team report on Coal Mining noted that a certain pride was taken in the coal districts that the Automobile industry has many ex-miners on its payrolls turning out cars which the active miners could afford to buy because of higher pay from mechanization. One instance was cited by the team members where a mine reorganization reduced the labor force from 900 to 600 men, with a substantial increase in productivity. Before the change the proposal was discussed with the operatives. At no time during the procedure was there any problem of union opposition. Eventually the displaced workers were reabsorbed elsewhere.[18]

In the opinion of the British Trade Union Officials there is no more eloquent example than Coal Mining to show the difference in rates of industrial output between Britain and America. The better natural condition of work and particularly the advanced state of mechanization in the American mines permit the miner to produce "four to five times as much per shift" as does the British miner. One of the reasons offered to explain the great support given to mechanization by the United Mine Workers is the keen realization of the economic vulnerability of coal in the face of competition from natural gas, oil, and hydroelectric power. The union maintains it is better to strive for utmost competitive efficiency, offering good wages and working conditions to a declining number of workers, than to attempt to provide employment security for a static work force with no heed given to the competitive situation faced by the Coal industry.[19]

The British team on the Coal Mining industry learned that more highly developed methods of production enabled considerably fewer miners in the United States to produce a given tonnage of coal with no greater effort than required in Britain, and for a much higher daily wage. As in other American industries, the team members found the strong conviction on the part of both workers and management that greater output at lower cost is the key to higher wages, shorter hours, and better working conditions.

Nevertheless, the Coal report emphasizes that certain natural advantages enjoyed by the American Coal industry are lacking in the British coal mines. The more convenient pillar system of mining is not possible in Britain since the coal veins now left in Britain are too narrow for this method.[20] Again the mine shafts in the United States are still comparatively shallow (averaging 190 ft.), and so additional ventilating shafts can be installed without too much difficulty. In Britain the mining surfaces are now so far below the earth (averaging 1,170 ft.) that adequate ventilation is a much more serious problem than in America. Many outcroppings of coal in the United States are found in valleys; this permits easy access to the work sites. The team reported that actually only 25 percent of the American output is raised in shafts. Horizontal hauls from the mining face to the surface are possible for the major portion of the coal mined. This circumstance makes it worthwhile to invest more heavily than in Britain in mechanical methods of boring.[21]

The report of the productivity team representing Freight Handling contained an instance where mechanization did not get the customary response from the union. At one port terminal it was found that the union representing the stevedores, while not opposed to the introduction of mechanical equipment, refused to accept any cut in the number of basic gangs of workers despite the greater output per man as the result of mechanization. Actually this position taken by the union did not greatly annoy some of the employers since workers were paid on an hourly basis and with the same wage outlay after mechanization a greater volume of freight was moved by each man.

In regard to the longshoremen, or those engaged in hauling to and from vehicles, employers were able to reduce work forces after mechanization without opposition. In general, team members covering Freight Handling, who visited numerous terminal and loading points in each of ten American cities in 1950, found that in the ports visited mechanical devices are used widely. Moreover, this development took place with comparatively little opposition from workers. It was regarded as another instance of technological progress which both employers and workers considered as inevitable.[22] In the case of freight depots, use of mechanical handling devices by agreements with the unions, while causing some displacement of men initially, increased the volume of freight handled by the depots so greatly that new workers had to be hired in addition to the recalled employees.[23]

The Union Contract

In the view of the British team which visited the Brush industry in the United States, the union-management contract in America permits considerable security for the worker and gives the union a more definite status within the plant than is true in Britain. This team noted that the typical union agreement not only concerns conditions of employment but also embraces provisions on social services.[24] A frequently recurring clause noted by the Brush industry team and by the team covering the Valve industry was the stipulation that there would be no strike or lockout during the life of the contract.[25]

On the matter of content the British team covering the Munitions industry noted the variety of conditions placed in the agreement by management. Such stipulations included the assurance that management shall retain the prerogatives and functions recognized by law and that the exercise of any of these rights and functions shall not be a matter for arbitration. The contract also sets forth conditions relating to discharge and discipline.[26] A clause accepted by the union states that in most circumstances it will not call or support a work stoppage, a "slowdown," or picketing as long as the contract is in effect. The British team visiting the Steel Construction industry noted that standard provisions of American contracts dealt with wage rates, grievance procedure, seniority, holidays with pay, and health and safety.[27]

On the less favorable side, after studying a number of union agreements in the Pharmaceuticals industry, the British team covering this area concluded that the considerable detail in these contracts must induce excessive rigidity in plant negotiations. This team regarded it as paradoxical that while personal relations in American plants are quite informal, collective bargaining situations have become decidedly rigid.[28]

In contrast to the criticism by the Pharmaceuticals team, it was the belief of the group studying the Internal Combustion Engine industry that union agreements in America make for simpler negotiations than in Britain. This team noted that instead of a plethora of such contracts relating to various divisions and classes of labor, so frequently

found in British firms, there existed for all practical effect
only one agreement throughout an American plant.[29] Also
stressing the note of simplicity, the Grey Ironfounding
team was impressed by the clarity of language found in the
union contracts studied. Members of the team gave this
factor much weight in attributing credit for the sound relationship between workers and management in the Grey
Ironfounding industry.[30]

A contrast between British and American union agreements was noted by the Meat Packaging and Processing
team. It was observed that once a contract was signed between a company and a union for a definite period, no
further demands for ordinary wage increases or changes
in working conditions were admissible during the life of
the agreement. In Britain the team pointed out that a contract on wages and working conditions does not usually
specify the period of duration and accordingly additional
demands may be presented at any later time.[31]

Members of the Food Canning team saw an advantage
in the provision for a fixed wage period in the American
type of contract. It permits an employer to determine his
forthcoming labor costs and thus he can achieve a more
satisfactory budgetary check on his business.[32] Nevertheless, it was noted by the Munitions team that while contracts frequently are in effect for one, two, or three years,
the present tendency is to keep the number of years to a
minimum in view of the constant spiral of living costs. True,
in some agreements adjustments for change in the cost of
living are permitted during the life of the contract.[33]

While maintaining that the usual contract of employment in an American furniture plant seems more complex
than the national agreement for the British Furniture industry, the British Furniture team was impressed by the

simplified presentation of the contract in the booklet given to operatives. It was noted that illustrations were used in this publication to point out the more important phases of the terms and conditions of employment.[34]

The British team which visited the Cakes and Biscuits industry regarded the American labor agreement as unusual in the light of British experience. Members of this team were interested to learn that it is in effect a legally binding document regulated in a number of ways by the Labor Management Relations Act of 1947. For this group long familiar with bargaining methods and practices prevailing in Britain, collective bargaining in America seemed to be unduly hampered by legal decisions bearing on definitions and interpretations. The end result appeared to involve less flexibility than is found in British collective bargaining. Some compensation for this greater rigidity, however, was seen in the number of guarantees of benefits often written into American labor contracts.[35]

UNION BUSINESS AGENTS

Unlike the situation in Britain, the report of the team visiting the Brush industry considered that the business agent representing a union in America had a position of considerable status within the factory organization. He was even compared to the personnel officer in large British concerns. In the opinion of the team members, the American business agent is well aware of the importance of the profit motive and appreciates that the assurance of good conditions for members of the union depends on prosperity for the employer.[36] In the report of the team studying the Food Canning industry note was taken of the extensive power exercised by this local union official in America. It was found that he had the exclusive right to conclude a contract on behalf of the union members in a factory and to represent them before management. In many contracts the team members learned that the union business agent has express authorization to handle affairs of the union. In one factory they noticed an office especially provided for his use.[37]

SHOP STEWARDS

It was the view of the union-management team covering the Munitions industry, that shop stewards who represent the union within the plant itself enjoy the same status which is accorded them in Britain. The union simply informs the company annually that certain individuals have been elected to act as union stewards in the various departments. These union representatives in turn elect a chief steward and an executive committee. In the larger plants it is customary to permit the chief steward to give his full time to union affairs. An office is provided for him by the company. However, his wages come from the union. In smaller companies only part of the day of the chief steward is taken up with union matters. The part of his time at his regular job is compensated by the company and the remainder is charged to the union, that is, time given to negotiations and grievance procedure.[38]

LOCAL AUTONOMY

The specialist team on Welding found that there is a substantial difference between collective bargaining in the United States and in the United Kingdom. It was the team's observation that very few American unions, related to manufacturing, bargain on what might be called a national scale. Moreover, even in exceptional instances such as the coal, steel and auto unions, national influence was confined to certain broad phases involving issues of general wage increases, pensions, or health insurance. For the most part the members of the Welding team considered that plant level collective bargaining prevailed with special attention to the consideration of local conditions. It was surprising for the British team to find on one occasion that two local unions of the same international were doing the same type of work in two different plants, but under divergent wage patterns and working conditions. Nevertheless, the Welding team report did note that such local inconsistencies are rapidly disappearing.

In general it was found that local unions possess an impressive degree of autonomy and are empowered to make agreements with local management as long as there is no infringement of policy laid down by the international union.[39] Moreover, the Welding team believed that save in an indirect way, a local plant union is not much concerned with other plants. One advantage seen in this situation was that employees of highly efficient companies do not suffer out of deference to less efficient firms. In effect it was believed that a closer spirit of co-operation and oneness of interest prevailed between unions and management because of this local autonomy.[40]

Yet after describing the minute detail which characterizes local plant negotiation, the British team visiting the Internal Combustion Engine industry expressed preference for the British method of negotiation on a national basis. Nevertheless, the team remarked on the profound knowledge of company problems possessed by union officials, which was obtained by dealing first hand at the plant

level. The British visitors did not deny that such understanding might aid in maintaining better relations than if
negotiations were carried on only at the national level.[41]

As a criticism of local bargaining, the British team
studying the Machine Tools industry commented that the
practice of localized bargaining is nicely adapted to the
policy of dividing the opposition. The team members believed this local approach, however, might redound to the
disadvantage of workers in time of depression. To illustrate
the divisive technique the Machine Tools report considered that at time of renegotiation each plant for all practical purposes is on its own in dealing with the union. A
strike may break out at any time during this period. Accordingly the team members concluded that localized
bargaining does not fulfill the claim that it is a protection
against strikes. Though conceding that national negotiation as carried on in Britain is rather unwieldy, the team
members saw in it a stabilizing influence on the economy.[42]

SENIORITY

Layoffs by seniority, a procedure chiefly sponsored by
unions to apply when work forces are reduced because of
mechanization or recession, received a mixed response
from several productivity teams from Britain. The report
of the Steel Founding team considered the practice as opposed to the maintenance of the most efficient work force.[43]
Members of the special Welding team found the seniority
rule to be rigidly enforced and fraught with several in-
flexible provisions. This team learned that not only employers but even certain trade union officials expressed
public and private opposition to the practice. The team
members believed it could act as a deterrent for young

people to enter factories. The Welding team felt that the enforcement of the seniority rule in time of depression could put a work force in a low state of efficiency by retaining only the older men and at the very time when highest productivity was essential to keep down costs. With some degree of naiveté the Welding report characterized the seniority rule as most inconsistent with the vaunted boldness and vigor of American enterprise.[44] Representatives from the Internal Combustion Engine industry also regarded rather doubtfully the wisdom of the seniority rule in deciding the order of layoffs in time of slack work. They noted that in Britain decisions of this nature were entrusted to the discretion of management which in their estimation was guided by the comparative fitness and efficiency of the different workers.[45]

An instance where a British productivity team felt that the seniority rule had been carried to extremes was in Brockton, Massachusetts, a Footwear center. The team covering this industry stated that since no pension or retirement age is observed, the average age prevailing in the Brockton factories is much above that of any other area visited in the United States. In effect the older workers are permanent employees while the younger operatives can be regarded merely as temporary. The only factors which can remove the grip of the older generation on this industry in Brockton is voluntary withdrawal, sickness, or death. The Footwear team report suggests that this rigid enforcement of the seniority rule in the Brockton area may help explain the migration of the Shoe industry to the Western states.[46]

The British report on the Pressed Metal industry declared that the entire scope of American labor conditions is vitally influenced by the seniority system and to a degree

almost unknown in Great Britain. As examples of some of
the unfavorable results from seniority the Pressed Metal
team noted the following: in the case of layoffs, merit
yields to service; the senior operatives are in a position
practically to choose their own jobs; a feeling of frustra-
tion may characterize younger workers; regular work may
become quite remote for a man who loses his seniority;
fear of losing seniority may keep workers in blind alleys
and thus lessen their desire to improve their status.[47]

While noting that knowledge, training, skill, physical
fitness, and efficiency are taken into account in cases of
promotion or transfer, the report of the Electricity Supply
team concluded that primary regard is given to departmental seniority. It was the general observation of this
team that no claim to promotion is based directly on apprenticeship, training, scholastic record, or on experience
gained outside the firm. In other words new entrants must
start at the bottom and their progress is normally governed
by length of service and demonstrated ability. It was noted,
however, that each employee was urged to qualify for the
next step in line of promotion and to regard himself as eligible for that post.[48]

The special report by British Trade Union Officials acknowledged that certain merits could be seen, nevertheless,
in the practice of seniority. Two such points would be that
it tends to restrict favoritism and it safeguards employment
for workers who might have difficulty getting a position
elsewhere because of their age.[49]

Members of the Electric Motors team were inclined to
approve the rule of "last in, first out" at the time of layoffs.
Instead of seeing it as a blow to initiative, this team regarded the seniority system with its emphasis on high
ratings as a strong incentive for workers to seek better

positions as protection against "bumping." In effect they saw the grading system associated with seniority as a method of classifying workers according to merit.[50]

The team representing the Boxes and Carton industry, which covered sixteen American factories in 1950, recommended in its report that some thought be given in Britain to the use of the seniority rule on questions of privileges and promotions. It was asserted in the team report that the seniority rule induces workers to earn the highest possible seniority rating through promotion to better jobs, and this in itself would aid productivity.[51]

Members of the Furniture productivity team after commenting on the fact that seniority dominates not only in case of layoffs but also in regard to transfers and promotions within the plant suggested that such a rule might help to maintain a low labor turnover. This result would seem to follow since senior employees have first choice of positions within the factory provided they have the necessary ability.[52] A similar view was taken by the team studying the Dairy industry in the United States. It was the conclusion of this group that a well defined seniority system would contribute to greater productivity by an improvement of working conditions and through reduction of labor turnover.[53]

WORKER MOBILITY

In summarizing their findings the fifteen members of the Valve team observed that entrance even to a skilled trade in America is open to anyone, including a middle-aged worker, if he shows capability after suitable training. The actual serving of an apprenticeship is not required.

Moreover, there is no formal barrier preventing a man from changing his occupation.[54]

Encouragement of worker mobility was seen by the British team on Welding in the entrance rules of American unions. Even where the union shop is in force, it was noted that the employer is free to try out the new worker for thirty days before he must join the union. In the observation of this team, the American working population is highly fluid and man power can readily move from plant to plant as economic fluctuations may warrant.

Contrast was made with the situation in Britain where most unions require that a prospective employee must already possess the proper card showing membership in a particular union or even a subdivision of it before he may begin work. Further, in the case of British craft unions an additional qualification is required that the applicant has served an apprenticeship of five years. In effect this latter regulation tends to restrict the supply of craftsmen at a given time to the intake of apprentices many years before when economic conditions might have been much less favorable. True, in times of emergency some dilution of the rules is permitted by mutual consent, but only after ascertaining that no fully trained craftsmen of the particular union are available in the area. It was pointed out that re-employment of workers in America can take place immediately without negotiation between unions and management. Generally the members of the Welding team believed that British craftsmen tend to regard themselves as permanently associated with one particular trade because the requirement of a new apprenticeship prevents taking out membership in a second union.[55]

A quite different appraisal of labor mobility in America

was made by the Cotton Yarn Doubling team during the visits to Northern and Southern mills. It was the conclusion of this team that workers in American cotton mills are no more mobile than in Britain. From this team's observation it is an exceptional case when an operative is transferred to a different process or job. Since an ample labor supply makes it possible to engage new workers when necessary, no effort is made to train operatives for more than one job in a given plant. The team members did not deny, however, that workers in many mills are able to do several types of operations because of experience gained in other firms.[56]

UNION RESEARCH DEPARTMENTS

A constructive approach toward the adjustment of union membership to new methods of production can be found in the experience of unions with industrial research. The report by British Trade Union Officials notes that the establishment of research departments in American labor organizations has been a rather recent development, coinciding with the expansion of industrial unions. It is believed that the large scale impact of scientific management, which came with the full flowering of mass production, has necessarily spurred the resort to union research. Since industrial union leaders are aware that the techniques of scientific management, which actually may be unscientific at times, are becoming more widespread and accepted each year, they see the need for some institutional device such as research to prevent abuses and to guide developments.

Nevertheless, the British Trade Unions' team pointed out in its report that even today American craft organizations prefer not to concern themselves with production problems to the extent of engaging in research.[57] By contrast, an industrial union such as the Textile Workers' Union believes it has a special responsibility to persuade both workers and employers to make use of every means which will increase productivity. Toward this end it has established a research organization to publish for its members pamphlets and directives on technical phases of production. Union officials have used this material to urge employers in their areas to make improvements both in methods and in machinery.[58]

1. Textile Workers' Union

The T. U. C. report on Trade Unions and Productivity states that the Textile Workers' Union was one of the first labor organizations in America to establish a research department. It is staffed with personnel who have special training in such fields as economics, engineering, management, publicity, and law. Data gathered by this research department touches upon the financial, industrial, and labor records of companies in the industry. Specific information is on file in regard to problems of work loads, and labor costs. The broad economic characteristics of the Textile industry and general industrial and bargaining policies of employers are studied. As a result the research department enables the officials of the Textile Workers' Union to determine the ability of particular companies to pay wage increases and to detect instances where the union should seek to improve the industrial structure of certain companies.

In the course of collective bargaining members of the research department of the Textile Union often come to the aid of local officers who are not versed in the latest

techniques of scientific management. In effect this department has made a notable contribution to the development
of union policy on such matters as merit rating and time
study. It has enabled the union to show how managements
can cut costs by improving efficiency instead of resorting
to wage cuts. Organizers receive special training from this
department on matters of job specifications and work
duties. The department maintains a careful record of all
case histories of production engineering in which it has
participated.

Another service of this department is to provide union
officials with current information on changes in the tech-
nology of the Textile industry. On this point revolutionary
changes have occurred since World War II which have
transferred to mechanical devices most manual operations
in regard to lifting and handling. A more technically
versed operative is now required.[59]

2. *International Ladies Garment Workers' Union*

The management engineering department of the International Ladies Garment Workers' Union is another outstanding instance of research carried on by a labor organization. This department endeavors to be thoroughly
versed in the different aspects of scientific management
for two reasons. It is necessary to keep management aware
of the practical limitations of this technique; and secondly,
in collective bargaining the tools of industrial engineering
must be familiar to union officials in order to negotiate
wages and work loads. Careful recruitment of staff for this
department is stressed so that the aims and values of the
union will be safeguarded. From past experience the union
has found it unwise to employ college-trained engineers

with no previous union experience. Now the procedure is to select actual trade unionists for training in industrial engineering.

Keeping in mind the importance of high productivity as a basis for high worker income, this department of the I. L. G. W. U. offers aid to employers who lag behind from lack of better techniques in manufacturing and operation. Often at the request of a local union, the Management Engineering Department of I. L. G. W. U. will inspect a plant and make recommendations and suggestions. The department also maintains a library of uniform data related to labor operations in all branches of the industry. The ultimate aim here is to standardize an ideal time period for all types of manual operations throughout the Ladies' Garment industry. To this end a complete laboratory on time and motion studies is in operation. A film library on the best methods of work performance is used for training union members. While the union refrains from actually installing production systems, it demands on such occasions that a committee representing the union research department, the management, and the local union accompany the commercial industrial consultant who is in charge of the installation.[60]

3. United Automobile Workers

The last of the three unions in America which the report of the British Trade Union Officials cited for having management engineering departments in the strict sense is the United Automobile Workers, C. I. O. The main concern of the Autoworkers in regard to research relates to the determination of the amount of effort expected of members. The U. A. W. is not opposed to the installation of laborsaving machines, nor does it attempt to set the number of machines to be operated by one man. If the union and the operative find that new methods simplify certain work to such a degree that without extra effort one man can operate three machines instead of one, no objection is raised. For recompense the union endeavors to bring about an annual wage increase of an over-all nature based on technological increases in productivity.

As in the case of the Garment and Textile unions, the U. A. W. finds it necessary to be thoroughly conversant with time study methods so that any fallacies can be speedily detected. The Time Study and Engineering Department at Detroit is staffed with men trained at production engineering colleges. This department comes to the aid of locals seeking information concerning standards of production, job evaluation, and incentive plans. Besides furnishing general information on time study methods, the department also trains local union representatives in acceptable procedures of time study.[61]

In close relation to the Engineering Department, but operating in broader economic and industrial areas, is the Research Department. Similar to the research work of the T. W. U., the U. A. W. Research Department makes analyses of the financial status of many companies covered by U. A. W. contracts. Locals may obtain from the Research Department data on wage rates for operatives of particular machines in other plants. This department maintains a punched card system for the various contract clauses which have already been negotiated and they can thus serve as precedents for future contracts. By means of the department's service, new developments on general economic problems are frequently brought to the attention of the officers and members of the U. A. W., as well as to the public. Instances can be cited by the U. A. W. where the efforts of the Research and Engineering Departments have enabled small scale, inefficient management to meet demands for pay increases by following U. A. W. suggestions for increasing productivity.[62]

The report of the British Trade Union Officials also refers to other unions in the United States which carry on research, but in a more restricted sense than is true of the three unions mentioned above. Reference is made to the United Steelworkers of America which operates a special research department to furnish economic statistics and information bearing on wage problems. Officers of steel locals find this department a source of help when the companies with which they deal present peculiar circumstances requiring special adjustments. The Inequities Department of this same union is staffed with competent production engineers who assist locals occasionally on technical phases of negotiation.[63]

The International Association of Machinists operates a well organized research department staffed with professional personnel. However, the I. A. M., unlike the policy of the I. L. G. W. U., endeavors to obtain this personnel from among the trade union membership already possessing college degrees. Though basically a craft union, the I. A. M. has a considerable non-craft membership and holds contracts with 10,000 employers in regard to jobs involving over 2,000 classifications.[64] The United Garment Workers maintains a research and production engineering department largely for the purpose of settling disputes concerning piecework. The union considers that the best way to protect the union member and to insure his economic improvement is by careful study of individual productivity.[65] In the case of the United Mine Workers, union officials by detailed knowledge keep currently informed on the latest methods of production in the Coal industry. This data enables them to evaluate the possibilities and limitations of the new technologies in the industry.[66]

The research department of the Amalgamated Clothing Workers, according to the British Trade Union officials, has an extensive program and is staffed with production engineers capable of reorganizing work flows and simplifying work processes. The union is well aware of the need for substituting machinery at times for manual labor. In such cases the union seeks some form of compensation for the displaced workers such as "dismissal pay." Aid is also given these workers in finding new employment. The A. C. W. is noted for its broad research programs on economic problems and for its promotion of life and health insurance by actual operation of such programs for its members. The research department has also made intensive study of family budgets in various industrial areas to determine how average hourly earnings correspond with the incomes necessary for a minimum living standard.[67]

Union Structure

The extent to which unions even in the American Federation of Labor have become adjusted structurally to the demands of assembly line methods of production is indicated by an analysis of membership cited in the British Productivity report on Welding. This report notes that many American unions which formerly were craft in structure have to a great extent become industrial or semi-industrial unions. The report stated that in all the A. F. of L. unions, only one-sixth of the members by 1951 were in strictly craft and multi-craft unions. About one-third of the membership in A. F. of L. unions belonged to extended craft organizations which accept not only skilled workers, but semiskilled and unskilled as well. Approximately one-half of the total A. F. of L. membership belonged to industrial and semi-industrial unions.

While the C. I. O. began as a federation predominantly of industrial unions, it has at times made use of "special" locals to meet the requirements of strong craft groups. Since the development of full scale mass production, however, strict craft unions have become a declining minority in the United States. An intriguing discovery made by the Welding team was that some unions have a sort of chameleon character by which under certain conditions they operate as craft unions and in other cases as industrial unions. Examples of this type were found among the carpenters, teamsters, electrical workers, boilermakers, and machinists. The British report on Welding suggests that in view of the high productivity quotients in America and the part unions have contributed here, it might be well to study future possibilities for the industrial union in the United Kingdom.[68] The British Furniture team report states that the adjustment of American unions to the waning of apprenticeship and the breaking down of work processes enables management to select about any worker who wishes employment in industry. No barrier to union membership stands in his way and once his particular task is mastered, usually in a few weeks, he becomes a fully accepted member of the union and the industry.[69]

It appeared from a study of union structures that the regulations and administration of unions in America are much broader and more flexible than is the case in Britain. The Welding team saw in the American approach to unionism more of a stress on improvisation than an adherence to abstract principles of organization. Under the rule of the National Labor Relations Board it seemed to the British that a union seeking recognition would be willing to organize along craft or industrial lines depending on the bargaining unit.[70]

Nevertheless, a startling example of traditional craft unionism pushed to extremes was encountered by the Footwear team on its trip to Brockton, Massachusetts. In the shoe factories visited there the British found fifteen separate locals of the same parent union. Contrary to this situation the Footwear team pointed out that in Britain the trend is toward the reduction of unions and branches of unions in order to promote unity of interest. While acknowledging the importance of highly skilled operations in manufacturing, the British Footwear union is opposed to division of interests between groups of workers in the same department or plant. Accordingly the Brockton situation was regarded as anomalous, where fifteen branches of the same union in one factory hold separate meetings, maintain independent staffs, and present different claims to management.[71]

While the members of the Welding team realized that the industrial form of union does not serve as an automatic safeguard against jurisdictional disputes, called questions of demarcation by the British, they believed such disputes were resolved more quickly where there was only one union in a factory.[72] The productivity team report on the Furniture industry, however, cited an involved situation where an industrial union, the U. A. W., had won jurisdiction in a furniture factory. As a result a union chiefly associated with the Automobile industry handled negotiations with a company producing not only metal seating, but also church furniture, panelings, and wooden seating as well.[73]

UNION ATTITUDE TOWARD MANAGEMENT

Though the members of the productivity team on Coal were aware of the turbulent history of bitterness and violence which existed in the American Coal industry over the last thirty years, the team believed that out of the strife has come a keen awareness of the functions and responsibilities of both union and management. While workers and employers are in the Mining industry for different ends, they see that increased efficiency is the path which both must follow. Of the twelve mines visited by the team members, labor relations at the actual working sites seemed free of tension and bitterness. The British Coal experts, however, realized that the area visited marked only a small portion of the industry.[74] In general the impression gathered by the Coal productivity team was one of constant struggle at the national level and somewhat friendly though vigilant co-operation in the coal fields as such.

Members of the Non-Ferrous Metals team found that both employers and workers whom they encountered in America were in agreement on the view that more output per manhour means lowered cost, greater purchasing power, and greater demand for goods. The British visitors regarded this attitude to be in sharp contrast with the opinions of certain people in Britain who fear that the consequence of greater output can only be redundancy of workers.[75] Making a similar finding, the report of the productivity team on Welding also indicates that in the areas covered by this team, members were impressed by the common realization of management and unions that economical production was a basic requirement.[76]

American trade union officials in the Internal Combustion Engine industry told British representatives that the union realized it had to work together with management in the interest of all. Realization was acknowledged that more was to be gained by compromise and cooperation than by warring with management. Members found actual evidence of the openness in attitude which prevailed between employers and unions in some of the plants visited by this team.[77]

British representatives covering the Brassfoundry industry concluded that both management and workers have a decided respect for each other's capabilities. Both groups are aware that each would be handicapped without the other. Team members remarked at the personal understanding often existing between worker and employer, even between an employer and a trade union.[78] They saw no indication of class bitterness toward the executive in the factory, the man with authority to direct others. Workers accepted the fact that this directive ability was a rare and valuable asset in the factory and worthy of high compensation. Improvements in production authorized by the executive often meant larger wages for the operatives. Reversing the picture, the team members found that executives realized a lack of confidence in them by the workers would go far to nullify success for the best laid plans. Accordingly American executives gave indication that they appreciated the necessity of sharing the benefits of improvements with workers in terms of better wages.[79]

Industrial experts covering the Rigid Boxes and Carton

industry were impressed not only by the knowledge of the operations and machines possessed by trade union officials, but by the friendly situation existing between unions and management in this industry. Here was found an active two-way system of communication between management and workers, in large part due to able union officials and of mutual advantage at times of negotiations.[80]

While it was noted that a period of high prosperity prevailed in the United States in 1951, when the Packet Foods team visited America, members of this team remarked on the habitual friendly attitude between labor and management in this industry. The relationship in itself was regarded by the British visitors as a powerful influence for greater productivity.[81]

The Footwear industry made a sharp contrast to most of the findings of the productivity teams on the subject of union-management relations. The team covering Footwear plants found union organization in this sector not advanced to the same degree as in Britain. Moreover, great lack of uniformity was evident in the working conditions from factory to factory, due in part to the presence of independent unions, and the large percentage of unorganized workers.[82]

One of the reasons put forth to explain close relationship between management and unions in many American industries was cited by the specialist team on Welding. It was believed that the unions in America by allowing such great autonomy to the local organization at each plant encouraged a more personal association with management. The local in a sense has its present and future security tied up with the fortunes of one plant. This situation tends to encourage a mutual basis of interest with management.

The British Welding representatives were fully aware that disputes flare up from time to time, but this knowledge did not lessen the significance behind the ample evidence of mutual appreciation and confidence existing between management and unions.[83]

JOB EVALUATION

A notable example of union influence on management policy can be seen in the development of job evaluation and classification in the Steel industry. The British productivity team on Iron and Steel gave considerable attention in its report to this problem. A serious handicap to realistic collective bargaining experienced by the United Steelworkers, after winning recognition in 1937, was the widespread anomalies in the wage structure of the steel industry. Without logical basis, wages varied from job to job, from department to department, from plant to plant, even though in a great many occupations, working conditions differed only slightly.

Upon bringing this situation to the attention of the War Labor Board in 1944, a ruling was made that both union and management should begin co-ordination of efforts to devise a method of job evaluation which would permit a basis for an equitable wage structure. Acting on this order of the War Labor Board, a number of steel companies jointly drew up standard job descriptions for all the occupations in their plants. In turn these descriptions were accepted by the United Steelworkers' Union. For the purpose of grading jobs on the basis of compensation the companies and the union agreed that such matters as training, skill, responsibility, effort, and working conditions should be weighted according to a predetermined scale. To promote maximum uniformity in the Steel industry, an extensive range of jobs common to all iron and steel plants were accepted as standards.

The impressive accomplishment from this joint action of management and union was the reduction of wage classification groups from several thousands to 32 basic standard hourly rates. Long standing inequities in wage payments have been eliminated and the new job classification and wage structure are looked upon as a permanent improvement, subject only to minor modifications.

While it is true that the Steelworkers' Union, by no means accepts any job evaluation program as infallible, it believes that the present job and wage classification in the Steel industry goes far to bring understanding and ease of application into a wage structure previously weighted with grave inequities. In the view of the British Iron and Steel team, management also appeared to look with satisfaction on the results flowing from the new job and wage structure. The report of the Iron and Steel team, published in June, 1952, noted that the range then in effect between the highest and lowest paid workers in the American Steel industry was under 2¼ to 1.[84]

The British union-management team covering the Munitions industry went into some detail in describing the method by which American management and unions endeavor to work out job evaluations. The team members noted that job description and classification, proposed by the company, are submitted to a designated union committee. If approval is expressed, several copies of the submissions are signed and sent respectively to the top management and union office, the chief union steward, the industrial relation officer, the foreman, and the shop steward.[85]

UNION-MANAGEMENT COOPERATION—
POSITIVE AND NEGATIVE

An outstanding example of union-management co-operation on matters of time study was encountered by the team of British Union Officials when visiting an electrical plant in Detroit under contract with the International Brotherhood of Electrical Workers. Over a period of six years productivity in this plant had increased 36 percent. While, no piecework system is in effect, an incentive plan in the form of a "Productivity Reward" applies to each operative computed on the weight of output per man per hour.

Though a strike occurred in this plant in 1949, the year of the British team's visit, the dispute was settled after the union representatives admitted that revision of wage schedules was necessary in order to meet competition. At the request of the union officer, the company made available its cost accounts. A subsequent contract agreement included revision of wage schedules. Changes in methods of production were then instituted by the company and its competitive position enormously improved. The few operatives who were displaced were later reabsorbed. Introduction of an incentive plan caused earnings for workers to be greater than under the old wage schedules.[86]

Coinciding with the changes in methods of production, a joint production committee was established to handle issues arising from the new arrangement. Three members were selected by the union and a like number by management. It is noteworthy that the union executives preferred to appoint representatives for this committee rather than leave the choices to popular election of the local members.

Technical ability, in the opinion of the union president, rather than oratory would thus be the predominant factor in determining representatives for the committee.

The president of the local, who was on the payroll of the company, devoted all his time to union affairs within the plant in the capacity of a chief shop steward. Enjoying the full confidence of the membership, the local president was able to exercise considerable authority in regard to settlement of grievances. He was in a position to check on company time studies or participate in their computation. When complexities arose beyond the competence of the union local, staff members from the international's research department were called in as counsel.

In the estimation of the team of British Trade Union Officials, the solution of the wage dispute of 1949 by joint action of union and management was quite consistent with the preamble in the union-management agreement signed in 1948. This introductory statement recognized that security of employment, a mutual objective, hinges upon the ability of the company to maintain a strong competitive position. Both parties to the contract then pledged their effort to promote maximum efficiency and output.

Later, upon visiting the Bethlehem Sparrows Point shipyard in Baltimore, the British Union Officials found that the Shipbuilding industry seemed to offer less opportunity for the adoption of scientific management than is the case in the mass production industries. Moreover, there was little evidence of participation by the Union of Marine and Shipbuilding Workers, the recognized bargaining unit, in efforts to increase productivity. While the union here is of the industrial type and negotiates plant wide contracts, it has not succeeded in standardizing the basic rates in the Shipbuilding industry.

No organization was established in the yard to permit joint consultation on production matters between the union and the company. Further, a clause in the union-company agreement forbids any employee to engage in union affairs during working hours if the nature of the activity "interferes" with production. This negative attitude toward union activity in the yard emphasized the slight role accorded the union as a constructive force for increasing production. At any rate, in one phase of the yard's operations the union was permitted to participate, the Departmental Safety Committee. Quite unlike the practice in mass production industries where careful planning of work keeps the highly paid operatives constantly supplied with job assignments proper to them, the Bethlehem shipyard by a contract clause is free to assign craftsmen to do work outside their trade in order to eliminate idle time. While this provision may serve to assure a full workday from labor, it seems to do little to promote maximum productivity.[87]

The special team of British Union Officials believed that unlike some other industries, the employers themselves in the Building industry provided the main pressure for stepping up productivity. By careful planning of work and purchasing of materials contractors endeavored to maintain an even flow of production without delays. The part played by unions in expanding productivity, in the estimation of the British team, was concentrated on improving the skill of the building operatives and in showing a readiness to use new techniques, machines, and tools. Even so, it was noted that union restrictions do exist in some areas. For example, there are certain limitations on the extent to which paint spraying equipment may be used in the Building industry.

British Union Officials were impressed by the high standards maintained in the building trade schools in several of the larger cities. The Cleveland Trade School was noted in particular. This institution is operated jointly by contractors and unions with the co-operation of the Cleveland Board of Education and with the aid of governmental grants. An apprentice training school in New York organized by the International Brotherhood of Electrical Workers, and operated under similar conditions was also mentioned in the report of this productivity team.[88]

Despite the lack of "scientific method" equivalent to the degree found in the mass production industries, the productivity team on Building, which visited the principal cities in the United States between New York and Chicago in the summer of 1949, disclosed in its report that there is a margin of 50 percent in output per manhour in favor of the American building operative over his British counterpart. The significant factors accounting for this difference were the arrangement of job conditions to prevent wastage of time, the availability of unskilled workers to provide materials so that craftsmen may keep fully occupied on productive jobs, and stress on break down of craft processes to permit as much as possible repetitive functions for each operative.

Other conditions also were listed which the British team on the Building industry regarded as significant in explaining greater efficiency of American building operatives. It was believed that workers are less subject to fatigue in America than in Britain. Private means of transportation bring the American to his job more refreshed physically than the British workers who must spend considerable time on crowded, uncomfortable public vehicles. The plentiful supply of high quality food available to American workers also was regarded as an important factor in permitting them to maintain a steady pace throughout the day. Apparently it is not unknown for a worker in Britain to take time out in the course of the day from lack of energy because of a scanty breakfast or lunch.

Apart from these explanations however, the report of the British team on the Building industry stated that the superior productivity in America in large part can be accounted for by the attitude of the individual towards his work. As the British observer, Alistair Cooke, noted, it is only necessary to lean out of a window in a midtown section of an American city to become aware of the energy and intense application of construction crews during working hours. Though the quitting whistle disrupts their activities with the suddenness of an explosion, up to that time the air hammer, the electric drill, and the bulldozer are driven at a furious pace.[89]

The British Union Officials found little disposition in the construction industry to adopt the techniques of time study and job evaluation. Despite great strides in the use of mechanization and new materials, the skilled work performed in this industry remains largely unstandardized and thus beyond the reach of "scientific management." Though in some cities over 90 per cent of the operatives in building construction belong to unions, it was noted that the craft type predominated and in consequence approximately 30 unions are in the building trades.[90]

UNIONS AND POLITICS

Contrary to the situation in Britain, the members of the Welding team during their visit to America concluded that American trade unions are not of themselves a political party, nor are they committed officially to any party.[91] Nevertheless, there is a growing awareness on the part of unions in America of the need to gain the support and sympathy of the public in matters of negotiation with employers. As a result public relations are becoming highly developed and a number of unions now have their own radio stations.[92] In general it was the conclusion of the team of British Trade Union Officials that as long as the private enterprise economy in America continues to make possible a rising standard of living, the American trade union will not give much support to a program for a planned economy. Should a period of mass unemployment return, however, or if a sharp decline in living standards comes about, the British Union Officials would expect American unions to press for government public works programs along the lines of the T. V. A. Yet the degree of influence the unions could exert in a time of mass unemployment seemed a matter of conjecture.

Even during the boom period when the team of British Trade Union Officials was in America, evidence could be seen of a growing demand by trade unions for more political action, spurred on by the loss of purchasing power in the face of inflationary consumer prices. Because of this trend, it was thought possible that American unions may later assume a role of political responsibility similar to the trade union movement in the English economy. Moreover, the point was made that to the degree American unions persuade Government to shape the national economy so as to stabilize purchasing power, to that extent they will lessen the pressure on private management to meet these problems on its own.[93]

At the present time, in the judgment of the British team studying the Fruit Processing industry, the aims of American unions are quite nonpolitical. Moreover, the efforts of unions in America at election time seem to be directed toward supporting a particular candidate rather than a party. For all practical purposes no opposition along ideological lines is shown toward the capitalist system. The real anxiety concerns efforts to obtain maximum returns for union members under the present economy.[94]

SUMMARY

A generally constructive, realistic attitude toward labor-saving devices by American unions was noted in many of the British team reports. Chief union concern here related to matters of timing and adaptation. Unusual features for the British visitors in union-company contracts were no strike clauses and fixed periods for wage rates. Some reports found these contracts legalistic and rigid in nature. The authority of the local union business agent to negotiate and sign contracts appeared quite novel to the British teams. Members of the teams were impressed by the thorough knowledge of company problems shown by local officials. Some teams were quite critical of seniority procedures in regard to layoffs; yet it was acknowledged that American unions permit more worker mobility than found in Britain. High tribute was paid to the extensive research departments in the Automobile, Textile and Clothing worker unions. The scope of changes in union structure in recent years was shown by the finding that half of the membership in A. F. of L. unions is now industrial or semi-industrial instead of craft. The British teams concluded that union members here generally have a high respect for the efficiency of American management. While wary of its defects, a number of American unions regard job evaluation as a tool to improve collective bargaining and co-operate with management in applying it. In some indus-tries unions actively pressure management to improve methods; yet the more common tendency is to let manage-ment keep its own active pace in this area. The British teams found American unions not desirous of extensive government intervention in industry since the private economy is constantly expanding output. A severe depres-sion might alter this attitude.

CHAPTER FOUR

Wage Standards in America

Reference is made in this chapter to the comparisons made by a number of teams on the postwar picture of wages and consumer goods in Britain and America. The types of pressure exerted to increase wages in this country are noted. Findings from the team reports are given relating to the scope of wage structure in America, particularly in reference to national and local patterns, and intra industry differentials. To contrast living standards, a number of comparisons, drawn from the reports, are presented to show the amount of work time necessary to enable operatives from the same industry in Britain and America to buy similar consumer items. British comment is given here on the accuracy of the term "American standard of living." Observations from the team reports are mentioned as they bear on housing, diet, and taxation of wage earners.

COMPARISON WITH BRITAIN

By contrasting living conditions members of the productivity team for the Brassfoundry industry endeavored in their report to draw some comparisons between workers in Britain and those in the United States. It was emphasized that economic conditions of postwar Britain have not restored the incentive to earn which the American wage earner enjoys and which the British worker experienced before World War II. On their trip through the United States the members of the Brassfoundry team noticed that the average American seeks to acquire the material symbols of good social status and in doing so is not hampered by social taboos that would discourage certain personal acquisitions by British workers. Ownership of a car is commonplace for members of any income group. Good clothes and electrical devices for the home are not regarded as beyond the ordinary for wage earners. These circumstances all serve to provide the American worker with a strong incentive to earn.

By comparison the members of the Brassfoundry team drew a less attractive picture of the British situation in 1950, the year the team visited America. The British worker then was still under the pressure of controls placed on him during World War II, which have prevented accumulation of consumer goods in similar variety to those owned by American workers. While there was a beginning of a more prosperous trend for wage earners in Britain prior to World War II, austerity still predominated in 1950 despite over five years of postwar economy. The rate of production of motor cars even in 1953 made hope of delivery a remote possibility for most purchasers and in any case a heavy luxury tax had to be paid in order to operate a car. Utility clothing was insufficient and even food was limited. Unlike in America, the opportunity to enjoy more consumer goods did not serve as an impetus to greater output. Instead there was only the somber inducement from the need to produce more so that conditions would not get worse. The economic incentive which offers to Americans the attraction of a fuller and more enjoyable life was not manifesting itself in Britain to any marked extent even as late as 1953.[1]

The T. U. C. Report by British Trade Unions Officials points out additional differences between postwar conditions in Britain and America. The degree of wage restraint in the United States after the war has been much milder than in Britain. In England the unions found themselves facing a political position which made it necessary for them to advocate wage restraints. As a consequence, while many workers in America have enjoyed spectacular wage gains since World War II, earnings in Britain have been held in check.

The members of the team of British Trade Union Officials indicate that British unions by withholding demands for wage increases lost a control over management which has been very effective in the United States as a means to foster greater efficiency. In their report these union officials state that American unions through their wage demands force management to be more efficient in order to finance the wage increases. British unions under present circumstances, however, can only hope that if greater productivity is achieved, in some fashion, one result will be higher wages or lower consumer prices. Unfortunately, too large a section of management in Britain has been unwilling to adopt more efficient methods with only general economic pressures to spur them on.[2]

The report by the British Trade Union Officials, however, does not ignore serious problems facing British management which only remotely affect American industry. British manufacturers are geared to a scattered and varied market by reason of their great dependence on foreign trade. Production for the home market cannot be readily meshed in with production for export.[3]

British productivity teams put great stress on the favorable market conditions enjoyed by American industry. The large home market in the United States and the minor percentage of output going into foreign trade has made it less urgent in America to keep prices down in order to meet foreign competition. On the contrary because of Britain's great dependence on imports of foodstuffs and raw materials it has been imperative that English industrialists keep prices down to maintain a large foreign market for their goods.

WAGE POLICIES IN AMERICA

Little evidence was found by the British team of Trade Union Officials that difficulty from new production methods was used in America as an argument for wage increases. The typical arguments used for pay increases, in the estimation of this team, are capacity to pay, greater productivity, or the rising cost of living. According to the British team, American unions do not demand wage increases for their members on the basis of added strain from a change in method. It is preferred instead to request a simpler break down of the work process to eliminate the undue effort.[4]

The report on Trade Unions and Productivity notes that the International Ladies Garment Workers' Union opposes any efforts by backward employers to make wage cuts a cushion of resistance against stronger competition made possible by high plant efficiency. This union follows the policy of using as a standard for all companies the day rates and piece rates paid in the best plants. Promotion of such a standard in recent years has served to lessen considerably the existing interplant differentials and has raised the average wage rate for the industry. As a consequence every category of management has become sensitive to the need for greater plant efficiency and better methods of production in order to lessen aggregate costs of labor.[5]

WAGE STRUCTURE

The British productivity team representing the Welding trade noted in its report that hourly wages for this trade in the United States are unusually high as compared with British rates, averaging three to four times the prevailing rates in Britain. While it was acknowledged that the higher cost of living in America modifies this diversity somewhat, real wages still were above those in Britain.

Nevertheless the team on Welding noted that marked variations in wage rates prevailed in different districts in the United States. It was found that in the Welding trade the various occupations tended to be classified in three grades. Within each grade of occupation was observed a substantial wage range from low to high depending on the type of plant and especially the industrial region.[6]

On the basis of average weekly earnings for a large number of workers in the British Brush industry in April, 1950, it appears that American operatives in this industry averaging somewhat over $40.00 a week, were receiving almost three times the compensation of their British counterparts.

Furthermore, the work week in Britain amounted to 45.6 hours while the American work week was only 40 hours. Also, the members of the team covering the Brush industry pointed out that wages received by American Brush workers were comparatively low in relation to industry as a whole.[7] On this point the team on Welding believed that there was a much greater diversity in wage rates in the United States than in Britain with corresponding divergence in living conditions. As an example of a high wage group in America the Letterpress Printing team cited the basic wage rates in 1950 for hand compositors. The team members found that the New York operative received $90 for a 37½ hour week, while his British counterpart was paid 7 pounds for a 43½ hour week, roughly about $19.60.[8]

In regard to wage differentials for the various industries visited by the British productivity teams, the representatives of the Pressed Metal industry reported that the wage structure in this sector of manufacturing appeared to them to be much less complicated than in Britain. They found that frequently the management-union contract specified the wage rates applicable to each type of employee.[9] The team representing the British Coal Mining industry considered that labor relations had been greatly improved in American mining companies by the development of a national wage structure founded on day wages with moderate differentials between the various classifications. The widespread mechanization of the American Coal Mining industry had made possible this necessary improvement in wage structure.[10]

At present only 13 grades of underground workers are recognized and the wage of the highest paid worker is only about 25 percent above that of the lowest. An important reason for this narrowed differential is not just that wages of the lower grades have been increased but that mechanization has eliminated much of what was formerly lower paid work.[11] A somewhat similar explanation was made by the teams visiting the Internal Combustion Engine industry in the United States. In their estimation the term "unskilled labor" is rather misleading when applied to the American Engine industry since it means workers who have not had the full training embraced by a regular apprenticeship. Nevertheless, they found many in the "unskilled" category who were highly efficient though engaged in but one or a few series of operations. Furthermore, these operatives had survived a trial period of training in which others who did not come up to standard had been rejected.[12]

The team of British Trade Union Officials, however, found a much wider range of wage differentials among the eight grades of job classifications accepted by the International Association of Machinists. Between the highest and the lowest levels, that is, the toolmaker and the floor sweeper, a wage differential of 100 percent was noted. This variation was considered much greater than is the case with normal British wage differentials.[13]

Actually for the total range of worker income levels in the United States it was the belief of the British Union Officials that the average differentials between skilled and unskilled workers and between union and non-union labor is much broader than in Britain. Accordingly they considered that reference to an average wage in the United States conveys a less precise concept of the actual wage levels prevailing.[14] The report of this team stated that many union-management agreements authorized wage differentials where the range between highest and lowest rates amounted to 100 percent.[15]

The team covering the Building industry noted that in

the South unskilled labor, mostly drawn from the Negro population, received earnings far below the rates maintained in the North. It was observed, moreover, that the laborer in the Building industry, even in Northern areas, averaged only 65 percent of the wages received by craftsmen, though in Britain the comparable percentage is 80 percent. The team admitted, though, that a favorable effect of this greater differential in America is the ease of recruiting young men for the Building trades. Nevertheless, it was also pointed out that the high wage cost of craftsmen has compelled deliberate planning in building design to narrow the scope of craft operation as much as possible, and in certain types of construction to eliminate craftsmen completely.[16]

The team of British Union Officials found that there may be as many as sixty different wage rates in the same plant. Though at first impression it might be thought that these wage differentials were built up by careful job evaluation methods, the team found that in most cases the rates developed over a period of time and generally were based on an area pattern. The team conceded exceptions to this plethora of wage rates in the case of many Engineering plants. Here the recent Inequities Program sponsored by the War Labor Board in the Steel industry has greatly simplified wage structure. The fact, however, that wage negotiations for an entire plant are frequently carried on by a single union caused this team to feel that differentials are decidedly more rigid in the United States than in Britain. One union, according to the British Union Officials, has an easier time preserving a definite pattern of wage scales than is the case where several unions in the same plant are bargaining for the particular interest of their own members.[17]

The productivity team representing the Electricity Supply industry (Public Utilities) pointed out that only rare instances were found in the United States similar to the British practice of maintaining a fixed rate for each job. Instead the American custom favored periodic wage increases from a minimum to a maximum level for the same job depending on observed ability and results. Unions and management, after negotiation, state in their contracts both the amount of the potential increases and the time period between increases. The practice is not confined to skilled workers since laborers and helpers are similarly rated. The purpose of the periodic change in rates according to a set pattern is to compensate for acquiring greater knowledge of the job and to encourage further progress. General wage increases do not militate against this progression in rating for particular jobs.[18]

Representatives from the British Food Canning industry on their visit to this country in the summer of 1951 discovered that wage rates vary decidedly in this industry. It was found that wages were considerably higher on the West Coast where the seasonal aspect of the work is more pronounced. This situation was especially true in regard to the fish canning industry at Monterey, an area offering little alternative employment in the off seasons. Further, wages for women in this area were only slightly below the rate for men. All agreements, however, studied by this productivity team disclosed an extensive schedule of wage scales. In some contracts eleven grades of payment were recognized for men and six grades for women.[19] A less elaborate wage structure was found in the Cotton Spinning industry. The British team report for this industry states that as soon as a juvenile acquires the capacity to perform a given job, he or she receives the regular rate for that job, with no discrimination because of sex.[20] Of 26 job descriptions listed in this report the lowest paid job rated approximately 70 percent of the wage paid for the highest paid job.[21]

LIVING COSTS IN TERMS OF WORK TIME

To show that the higher wage rates in America were by no means cancelled out by higher living costs, the British productivity team representing the Building industry compiled a table of standard consumer items and expressed their London cost in hours of work for building craftsmen as a percentage of the cost in hours in New York. The comparison was based on British and American prices for November, 1949. The list represented such categories as foodstuffs, clothing, household goods, and entertainment. For bread, the London cost in hours was 160 percent of the New York figure and for tea, 360 percent. Men's shoes in London were 503 percent of the cost in New York. The price of a London cinema ticket was 304 percent of the New York cost. While American prices have risen considerably since 1949, it is unlikely that the advantage enjoyed in purchasing power by American consumers has been greatly lessened since income levels have also increased.[22]

Certain items as of 1949 were not much different in cost for both countries, according to the judgment of the team on the Building industry. For instance, members believed that the same proportion of the week's income was required for housing in New York as in London. Nevertheless, the markedly shorter time required to earn funds sufficient to buy most consumer goods in America astounded the members of the team on the Building industry. Furthermore, the team members remarked that despite this greater ease in acquiring adequate income to meet ordinary living expenses in the United States, there was no indication that American workers are inclined to be less desirous of earning even greater wages. Eloquent and unrelenting appeals to buy more goods have their effect on the American consumer.

Making a general comparison of the standards of living in the United States and Britain the productivity report for the Letterpress Printing industry noted that the 1949 consumer expenditure per capita in Britain was 99 (counting 1938 as 100), while in the United States in 1948, the latest figure then available, the value of individual disposable income was 152 percent of the 1938 figure. In effect the Letterpress Printing team judged the prevailing standard of living in Britain in 1949 to be barely the same as it was in 1938. Yet in terms of real income, obtained by balancing wages with prices, the living standard in America was 52 percent above the prewar figure. The team interpreted the higher purchasing power in this country as an indication of the degree to which greater productivity in America has reflected itself in a higher standard of living.[23]

The Furniture team endeavored to compare the cost of living for a skilled worker in America earning $100 per week and his counterpart in Britain probably earning 10 pounds per week. In terms of work time necessary to purchase commodities in the spring of 1951 it was found that in such categories as food, clothing, home care, luxuries, and transport, the British worker had to devote considerably more time to pay for consumer goods. Less work time, however, was required in Britain to pay for bread, telephone calls, and haircuts. Yet the cost in work time for clothing was three to four times greater in Britain. Expense for maintaining a car was over five times greater.

Home maintenance was only 30 percent greater in Britain than America. Cigarettes were classified as a luxury and the contrast between Britain and the United States in work time required to pay for this commodity was 8.8 to 1.[24]

In the opinion of the team studying the Grey Iron-founding industry, it appeared evident that an industrial worker in America is required to work less time than any industrial operative in Britain in order to pay for most commodities. Obviously the result means that the American worker has a higher standard of living, especially in terms of food, and clothing, and other basic requirements.

A comparative analysis of real values on the basis of work hours in London and New York, compiled by the National Industrial Conference Board in New York, was contained in the report of the team on the Grey Ironfounding industry.[25] The report explained that immediately after devaluation of the pound in 1949, the Conference Board sent a research group to London. It was the group's task to determine the prices of items in the budget for the average Englishman and then translate those prices into hours of labor necessary to buy the articles. The hourly earnings for the worker in New York were set at $1.417. For his London counterpart the hourly earnings were placed at 2/5½d, or roughly $.36 per hour in American money. There was approximately this same difference in earnings for foundry workers, a trade of particular interest to the members of the team on Grey Ironfounding. The average American member of this trade in September, 1949, earned $1.46 per hour, while the British foundry worker earned 3/1½d, or about $.44 per hour.

Using the New York cost as 100 it was found that most items in the categories of food, clothing, house furnishing, and personal needs required two to four times as many work hours to pay for them in London as was the case in New York.[26] For instance the Letterpress Printing team found from the table compiled by the National Industrial Conference Board that milk cost almost three and one-half times as many work hours in Britain than in New York. For shirts the work hours were over eight times greater in Britain. Bread was about the same in work time for both countries. A man's serge suit in London required over four times more work hours for its purchase than in New York. A radio required over seven times the work hours in New York.[27] Close confirmation of the findings of the National Industrial Conference Board study was made by the productivity team visiting the Diesel Locomotive industry in the United States. Their report states that to the team members it seemed evident that in terms of purchasing power the hourly wage rates of American workers are approximately equivalent to the purchasing power of British craftsmen who receive a bonus up to 300 percent.[28]

The productivity report on Brassfounding noted that for the year 1951 even articles that can be called essential were beyond the purchasing power of the British worker. For instance in the summer of 1951, while it was estimated that the average cost of a man's suit in hours of labor was about 39 hours in the United States, in Britain the estimate was 152 hours. Turning to high cost consumer items which would be considered in Britain clearly outside the category of necessities, members of the team for the Brassfoundry industry noted that it is possible for an average moulder in America to purchase a family car for the equivalent of 20 weeks' wages. A refrigerator would require the work time of three weeks for an American moulder, and a television set, two weeks.[29]

Lack of a General American Standard

The team of British Trade Union Officials considered that it is very difficult to make accurate comparisons of the standards of living in Britain and America because of a greater variation in the levels of income between organized and certain unorganized workers in America. Special mention was made in their report of the noticeable difference in hourly wage rates for operatives in retail stores, largely unorganized, as compared with workers in the well organized industries such as manufacturing and mining. Moreover, the pattern of consumption in all respects does not coincide in both Britain and America. For example, the team pointed out that weather conditions and distance between homes and work often put automobiles and electric refrigerators in the category of necessities. It was noted that of the 70,000 workers at the Ford plant in Detroit, 27,000 owned cars and each day traveled upwards of 40 miles each way between work and home. A similar situation was found to be true for coal miners who only by this long daily travel can avoid living in shabby mining towns.

Further proof that the average American worker is a difficult concept to use as a standard of comparison became evident to the British Union Officials when they noted the range of incomes in America for 1948. In that year 21 million families received incomes of $3,000 and over. However, incomes for more than eight million families were confined to a range between $2,000 and $3,000. At least four million families had incomes below $1,000 per year. It was pointed out that research carried on by the Amalgamated Clothing Workers of America showed that a family income of $3,000 per year in 1949 did not permit even some of the accepted necessities for the American family.

For example no provision for a car was possible with such income. In regard to clothing the head of the family could afford only one suit every two years, and an overcoat every six years. The wife in such a family could buy each year two rayon dresses, a woolen dress every five years, and an overcoat once in four years.[30]

The British report on the American Building industry, moreover, made clear that even an income of $3,700 a year after taxes in 1949 did not permit any great departure from a modest standard of living. This income was earned by a worker in Cleveland with a wife and two children. Actually it was based on earnings of $95.00 a week for approximately nine months in the year. Weather conditions prevented employment during the other months. For planning a full year's budget on this income it was necessary to set aside $25.00 a week against the three months of unemployment. From the $70.00 per week remaining another sum of $9.55 was put aside for savings. A further deduction of $11.15 was made to allow for expenses on car, clothing, medical care, and the like. Monthly outlays for rent, gas, telephone, electricity, union dues aborbed $20.05 of the weekly wage. Daily expenses for food, household supplies, gasoline, recreation, and personal needs required the sum of $29.00. The total of these expenditures amounted to $69.75 per week.[31]

After studying the question of comparative real wages in Britain and the United States, the members of the Building team regarded as an overstatement the commonly held view that high wage rates in America are made necessary because of the high cost of living in the United States. Confining their conclusions to employees in the

Building industry, the British team members reported that the proportion of earnings spent on necessities is lower in America and the general standard of living is considerably higher.

Commenting on the much discussed question of the comparative cost of living in Britain and the United States, the specialist team on Welding in 1950 acknowledged that while the higher cost of living in the United States to some degree offsets the higher wages, it by no means did so proportionally. The members of this team concluded that American employees are much better off than British workers. They noted, moreover, that despite the enormous wage outlay of American industry, it maintains a competitive position in world markets.[32]

Members of the Brassfoundry team dwelt on the many inducements to earn which daily have their impact on the American worker. They all appeared to be summed up in the term social status. According to the American meaning of this term, the Brassfoundry team would include in the expression: an attractive home, a family car, good clothes, and all the electrical appliances which make modern housekeeping free of drudgery. Stressing the fact that these hallmarks of comfortable living are within the purchasing power of most ordinary American workers, the British team members concluded that herein is a strong incentive to earn.

While acknowledging that workers in Britain just before World War II were beginning to enjoy a limited use of such products as motor cars and home appliances, the Brassfoundry report declared that this prewar position has not yet been regained. The British team members believed that insufficiency of housing, utility clothing, and foodstuffs, even though buttressed by cold figures on the ups and downs of production trends, do not provide the stimulus to earn which is so strong in America.[33]

DESIRE FOR BETTER STANDARD OF LIVING

The report of the team studying the Internal Combustion Engine industry in this country showed awareness of a prevalent longing by all groups in the United States for a higher living standard. This very aspiration was considered as an important motive in explaining the diligence and readiness for hard work on the part of so many employees in American industry. The British team believed that a force which tends to keep this desire for a higher standard of living constantly in mind is the enormous quantity and variety of consumer goods ever before the eyes of the American shopper. Members of this British team considered, however, that it is the American wife who really sets the pace for the worker in his unceasing quest for more and better consumer goods. In turn this influence sets up pressure for higher wages.

Considerable leisure time of the American worker is taken up with pursuits which require spending. Instead of devoting time to the cultivation of a garden, or some inexpensive hobby, many American workers seek commercial places of entertainment, and as they travel about even at night they find shops open which cater to the inclination to spend.

It was noted that the desire for a higher standard of living in America has been satisfied, after a fashion, even by those whose incomes were not quite up to the measure of their aspirations. The great development of installment selling in America, or what is called in Britain "hire-purchase finance," has made this possible. Members of the Internal Combustion Engine team found that in many instances a large proportion of the weekly wage was taken up by obligations incurred under installment purchasing.[34]

No great enthusiasm by the team members was shown toward the accepted preference by Americans for the latest gadget which in a short time would be discarded for its successor. Nevertheless, they regarded this attitude of Americans as important because of its effect on productivity. A magazine article was cited from a company house organ which brought out the contrast between Englishmen and Americans in their attitudes towards the new and the old. For instance an Englishman may take pride that his car is still serviceable after fifteen years of operation or that his house has been in use for 300 years. Yet Americans are known to discard personal possessions before they have lost their usefulness. The article readily justified this American practice on the grounds that the ceaseless desire for what is new and better improves the standard of living for all. For example, frequent purchase of new cars permits used cars in good condition to be more readily available for families in lower income brackets. The total market increases and private transportation becomes commonplace for the average American family. A disparaging reference to ancient houses in the article was countered in the British report of the Combustion Engine team by the statement that old houses can be almost as comfortable and easy to operate as some of the modern homes which were seen in America.[35]

Mention was made in the report of the Brassfoundry team of the belief that British workers attach more value to security and leisure than to a better standard of living. In contrast, the team members agreed that the average

American thinks in terms of earning more so that he may buy a home, a new car, a television set, or some other novelty. The report of the Steel Founding team was inclined to minimize the significance of this vaunted array of mechanical devices found in the American worker's home. Actually, some items which are apparently in the luxury class, such as refrigerators and automobiles, are in effect quasi-necessities because of American climate and travel problems. Further, the report noted that the cost in money of most necessities in the United States is much more than in Britain. The Steel Founding team was inclined to appraise the standard of living of at least the American foundry worker as not much above the British.[36]

HOUSING

While traveling throughout the South, the team studying the Cotton Yarn Doubling industry found that a considerable number of Southern mills were located in attractive villages owned by the mill companies. Originally a company would build a village and rent the houses to its employees. Many workers still occupy homes on such a rental basis. Through the check off from the payroll, rent and maintenance charges are collected. The team members learned that workers today are not compelled to vacate such houses upon leaving the employ of the mill. In at least one instance the management of the mill has set up a method whereby employees could purchase their homes on the installment plan.[37]

It cannot be said that the British team investigating Coal Mining in the United States was overly impressed by the housing conditions of American coal miners. While acknowledging that houses of miners ranged from the attractive to the squalid, the far greater number of such dwellings failed to indicate to the British visitors that the coal miner was the wage leader in America. The British report on Coal Mining recalls that communities for miners have tended to concentrate around the coal pits in the United States just as in Britain. Because of the permanent nature of the larger mines, the communities near them have taken on a more stable character by establishing schools, churches, highways, and community services.

Yet during the American visit note was taken that the trend is away from the company owned mining town, though many such communities still exist. Topography plays its part in explaining the location of present company coal towns. Few of them were observed in the Midwest where level terrain and good roads permit easy transportation. Moreover, the seasonal nature of coal mining in such states as Arkansas and Oklahoma, and the pressure for a second job has caused more miners to live in rural communities where extra work is available. Movement of industry and growth of population in certain areas of Pennsylvania and West Virginia have taken the coal miner out of his isolation, turning the former coal town into a mixed industrial community. Because of such trends, the coal companies have begun to sell their housing properties either to individual owners or to real estate firms.

In the Southern Appalachian coal regions company housing projects are still being built in locations remote from incorporated villages. The purpose is not so much to rent the homes as it is to attract a work force by offering modern dwellings to prospective employees at cost or close to it. No longer is it considered good policy by progressive coal companies to maintain dingy company towns as in the old days. This practice has too often been a source of ill will toward the employer and an extra burden for management.

Yet the old type company town has not by any means disappeared in regions where communications are poor and marginal coal companies are in operation. In such areas housing conditions can be found which are far below average. Here one sees unpainted clapboard shacks surrounded by muddy soil and filth. Nevertheless, the Coal team also encountered towns above the average where attractive homes were set amidst green lawns and well paved streets.[38]

The English visitors were pleased to learn that despite the impression to the contrary gained from American films, only a small percentage of American wage earners are tenement dwellers. Though the British Trade Union Officials found that most prewar detached or semi-detached homes were of frame construction, they noticed that there is an increasing trend toward the use of brick since the war. In sharp contrast to the British use of open fire heating, the Trade Union team learned that over 40 percent of American homes are centrally heated.[39]

In general, the housing problem does not present too serious an obstacle for worker mobility in America. According to the members of the Welding team, over considerable periods of time American workers will put up with housing conditions much below British standards, such as homes in trailer camps.[40] Another circumstance which was given considerable weight is that fact that so many employees in America drive their own cars and are thus in the habit of working in plants as far distant as fifty miles from their homes.

DIET

Members of the British team studying the Building industry in the United States remarked on the stamina of American workers which enabled them to maintain an even pace throughout the workday. This advantage was largely attributed to the abundance of high quality foodstuffs available at reasonable prices in America. It was noticed by these team members that when standard meals are not within a reasonable distance from a construction job, independent caterers frequently provide lunches by means of mobile canteens.[41]

After talking to American workers, the members of the team studying the Rigid Boxes industry concluded that wage earners in England consumed only one-fourth the fats each week which were in the typical American diet. These team members were impressed with the fact that workers in the United States ate as many as 12 to 18 eggs a week, as well as 3 or 4 pounds of meat. A favorable effect from the generous American diet was felt by the team members themselves in the increased supply of energy which they enjoyed as the weeks went on in the States. Despite the daily routine of walking through factories, slight fatigue was noticed even though a minimum amount of sleep was obtained each night.[42]

TAXATION

During a visit to this country in 1949 the British team representing the Rayon Weaving industry concluded that American workers felt the incidence of taxation to a much lower degree than was true in Britain. As a consequence there seemed to be less impairment of the incentive to earn in the United States.[43] It appeared, moreover, to the Brassfoundry team that direct taxes remain at a fixed percentage in the lower income levels and thus the natural inclination of the American worker to earn as much as possible is not discouraged.[44] Apparently from the comment of the Men's Clothing team a slight increase in the gross earnings of a British worker will place him in a considerably higher income tax bracket. Accordingly, he has little desire to expend greater effort just to pay more taxes.[45]

In the estimation of the Iron and Steel productivity team the average percentage of family income paid out in the form of both direct and indirect taxes is much less than in Britain. Comparing an American steelworker with his counterpart in the United Kingdom, the report of the Iron and Steel team conceded that a steelworker here who receives the average wage of his industry pays about the same proportion of income tax as his British counterpart. A skilled American worker, however, pays in taxes not more than half the proportion of his British equivalent, since British tax rates are much steeper for the more highly paid workers. In effect the graduated scale of income tax rates in Britain was considered to cut drastically any advantage going to the skilled worker because of higher wages. Even for the ordinary wage earner in Britain the weight of indirect taxes serves to cut down expendable income to a degree unknown in America.[46]

SUMMARY

Many of the British teams called attention to the attractive variety of consumer goods which tended to stimulate

American workers to earn greater income. Undue physical effort is rarely used as an argument for a wage increase by unions. Instead a demand is made for better job planning. British team members considered the spread of wage rates between unskilled and skilled occupations to be much broader in America than in Britain.

In 1949, it took two to four times more work hours to earn the price of many comparable consumer goods in Britain than in America. Since wage levels vary widely between organized and unorganized industries and between regions in the same industry, a number of teams regarded the term "American standard of living" as misleading. Though many workers now live in attractive detached homes, bad housing still prevails in many coal mining regions. The abundant, energizing diet common for American workers contrasted sharply with the lean fare available to British workers. The team members considered taxes on wage incomes as much lighter than is the case in Britain and that tax rates here do not cut in sharply on wage increases.

CHAPTER FIVE

Some Methods of Income Distribution

Here note is taken of the findings of British productivity teams on the attitude of American unions toward corporate profits and profit sharing. The extent and degree of success of incentive plans in various industries covered by the British teams receive attention. Good and bad application of piece rates, as presented in the team reports, are recorded. The different types of pension plans and welfare benefits, encountered in several industries by the teams form the latter part of this chapter.

UNION ATTITUDE ON PROFITS

The report of the productivity team on Building emphasized that under the private enterprise system in America employees tend to judge companies by the profits they make. Workers are inclined to associate themselves with

companies which make a larger profit and enjoy an established reputation. Such firms are considered to be more
efficient and more likely to provide constant employment
for highly productive workers.[1] A similar observation on
this point was made by the team of British Trade Union
Officials. Their report states that the attitude of American
unions to profits is consistent with the acceptance of the
capitalist economy by such unions. They do not regard
high profits, at least under competitive conditions, as a
social evil, but rather as an indication of efficiency and
high output per man-hour. American unions concentrate
their efforts on obtaining a fair share of such earnings. In
fact the most profitable company in an industry is selected
as the pace setter for bargaining purposes and the other
companies are requested to follow a similar pattern on
wages and piece rates.

The British Union Officials also stated in their report
that American unions realize that profitable companies
have the ability to pay high wages and frequently prefer
to do so rather than precipitate a strike which might en-
danger a promising market outlook. The less efficient companies, moreover, find themselves obliged frequently by
union pressure to maintain the same wage rates as the
most efficient firms. Accordingly the laggard companies
have no other recourse than to make less profits or bring
their efficiency up to the standard of the best companies.
It was noted that this competitive pressure has narrowed
to a relatively small degree the difference in efficiency between the highest and lowest rated companies in the
United States and therefore average productivity is high.[2]

Profit Sharing

In regard to sharing profits the report of the team on Fruit and Vegetable Utilization found that American unions in its area of investigation gave no encouragement to profit sharing plans. It was preferred instead that any extra return be added to the weekly pay rate and thus the members of the union would be assured a higher, regular wage free from the uncertainties involved in profit sharing.[3]

Nevertheless several types of profit sharing plans are in operation among companies in the United States. One system was described in the team report on the Footwear industry. Under this plan the John E. Lucey Company of Bridgewater, Massachusetts deposits annually in a local bank a sum equal to 25 percent of its profits prior to any tax deductions. The bank in turn credits each employee with a share in this deposit according to a definite formula. The entire fund deposited at the bank is under the control of independent trustees who have power to invest it and make payments to beneficiaries.

The number of units credited to each employee depends on his period of continuous full time employment. One unit of credit is due after 6 months, but less than 18 months service. At termination of service with the company, the employee is entitled to credits of past years. Ordinarily this money is paid over a period of five to ten years. If the beneficiary retires at 65, however, or is permanently disabled, the credit is paid in a lump sum. Payment is also possible through purchase of an annuity policy which in turn provides regular income to the beneficiary for the remainder of his life. Upon the death of an employee his estate receives a lump sum payment. In cases of hardship, a fractional payment of a credit may be allowed to a beneficiary.[4]

The report of the team on Meat Packaging and Processing describes the profit sharing trust plan of the Hormel Packing Company which was put into effect in 1944, following an amendment to the Internal Revenue Code. The plan is intended to build up a fund which will be sufficient to provide for retired employees. In years when profits are not made, however, no deposit shall be added to the fund. It is necessary to have a record of four years' continuous service before participation is allowed in the plan. As the years of service lengthen the rate of participation is increased. The company contributes on the basis of the ratio between net profits and sales or the net profit per hundredweight of sales tonnage, whichever permits a larger contribution for the year in question.

Another profit sharing plan also operated by the Hormel Company permits all employees who are on the payroll both at the beginning and end of the fiscal year to share in what are called joint earnings for that year. Computation of this figure is obtained by deducting from gross income all expenses of operation, but not the salaries and wages of employees eligible under the plan. The sum which remains is divided between employees and stockholders on the basis of a sliding scale. In effect, for the years when profits are low the percentage share going to the employees is greater. In years of high profits a smaller percentage share goes to the employees.[5]

INCENTIVE PLANS

Members of the team representing the Letterpress Printing industry gathered the impression that unions in the United States do not favor incentive plans of payment. The unions which this team encountered tended to discourage any differential in pay for individual workers, such as merit earnings. Extra allowance in pay rates is acceptable, however, for added effort required in a particular job, such as the case of a pressman operating an oversize press. Yet the union wage pattern makes no allowance, unlike in Britain, for the various types of keyboards operated by workers in the composing room. Operators on monotype or intertype machines, as well as hand compositors and readers, all work under the same wage scale and may be transferred at any moment from one type of machine to another.[6]

The Letterpress team found that wage payments based on output was the practice in some 10 non-union and open shop firms in this industry. One company had been operating such an incentive plan for 30 years and the method was regarded by management as most satisfactory. The report of this team noted that several of the Letterpress firms visited became union shops after 1935 and agreed as part of the contract with the union to drop their incentive payment plans. A number of these firms have since wished to reintroduce this method of payment. A company stated that after discarding its incentive plan, production declined 30 percent. It was pointed out, however, that by the use of other measures production has since been increased.[7]

From observations made by the team of British Trade Union Officials, it was concluded that incentive plans, whether individual, group, or on a profit sharing basis, are in operation in the United States to a smaller degree than even in Britain. Citing the U. S. Bureau of Labor Statistics as a source, the team declared that less than one-third of the labor force in American manufacturing is paid on the incentive basis. In general the British Trade Unions' team believed that American unions look upon incentive plans with considerable suspicion and, according to the industry, prefer in their stead either hourly wages or straight piece rates.[8]

After visiting over 15 Cake and Biscuit companies in the United States, the British productivity team representing this industry considered that perhaps the most unforeseen result of their investigations was the finding that in the American branch of the trade there was practically no use of payment plans based on results. This team, moreover, was told by the president of the Bakery and Confectionery Workers' International, A. F. of L., that he was unalterably opposed to the introduction of any incentive system. Members of the British team acknowledged that the high degree of mechanization, at least in the packing phase of this industry, might make it a dubious advantage to install an incentive plan for operatives whose speed is likely paced by machinery. Nevertheless it was the belief of these British visitors that biscuit packers in England work at a faster pace than similar operatives in America.[9] A tour of investigation through the Packet Foods industry in the United States by another British team also directed attention to the absence of incentive plans. It was remarked, however, that high standard weekly wage scales in America permit more abundant consumer purchasing than in Britain, even with incentive pay. Further, overtime premiums also help to swell the American pay envelope.[10]

Members of the team surveying the Rigid Boxes and Carton industry were made to realize that in those instances where incentive plans were in operation, there was no intention to permit sweatshop conditions to arise. Further, a number of cases were found in the course of the tour of investigation where incentive schemes were looked upon as obsolete and a source of discontent, both by management and by labor groups. In these instances it was the common view of management and unions that incentive plans induce excessive strain and bring about premature aging of workers. A justification given for the extensive use of incentive schemes in Britain at the present time was that while the United States has steadily increased its output per man-hour, Britain by 1951 had not yet restored the rate of output of 1938. Accordingly incentive plans were considered essential merely to attain a normal daily output.[11] It might be added that while the Rigid Boxes and Carton team urged in its report that incentive plans be installed throughout the United Kingdom, the members warned that care must be taken to establish these payment systems correctly in order to avoid great dissatisfaction later.

Decided coolness for incentive schemes was also encountered by the British specialist team on Freight Handling which in 1950 visited important freight centers ranging from New York to New Orleans. Members of this team were told by both unions and management that incentive plans induce overloading and overdriving of truck units, with consequent fatigue and a noticeable rise in the rate of accidents. At railroad terminals the team on Freight Handling found that, at least in the view of union groups, bonus schemes are not favored and management usually meets opposition whenever such a payment plan is proposed. It was noted that in the St. Louis area, covering 23 railway depots, only the New York Central terminal operates under an incentive plan. Even here the official position of the union is against the plan. It is allowed to continue only by tolerance of a long standing local arrangement. A few more exceptions to the rule exist in other cities.[12]

The report of the team covering the Internal Combustion Engine industry points out that incentive plans of themselves provide no assurance of top efficiency. For their effective operation it is necessary to check daily the operative's performance with the norm in order to detect immediately such faults as poor tools, incorrect methods, and unsuitable materials.[13]

By way of contrast to the findings above, many instances were noted by the British team concerned with Meat Processing where workers supplemented their regular weekly wages by a premium for extra results. Moreover, the British Meat Processing team found that in most of the plants the union organizations showed a co-operative attitude toward incentive plans, especially in firms where bonus payments have been in operation for a number of years. The report of this British productivity team indicated that the work standards are set in the Meat Packaging and Processing industry so that operatives are able to surpass the ordinary day-work performance by over 25 percent, and thus increase their earnings by a similar amount. The British investigators found that in practice workers were attaining in output about 20 percent over the standard.[14]

Of more than 20 plants visited by the British Furniture team in 1951 some type of incentive plan was found in all except three factories. Considerable variation, however, was found among these plans and no single method was regarded as typical. For the most part a group payment plan was in operation where several workers combine to bring to completion a particular process of production. In two furniture factories visited, both management and union officials expressed enthusiasm for the Scanlon Participation Plan recently adopted. Management believed that this plan encouraged a spirit of co-operation and co-partnership among the employees and increased the number of helpful suggestions received pertaining to production problems. In both cases, however, the plan was in operation for such a brief time that a "lieu bonus" was being paid until regular earnings would reach the predicted amount.[15] Most plants covered by the team investigating the production of Electric Motor Control Gear were operating under some form of incentive scheme. The plans included an individual bonus related to the time factor set for a given job as well as a group bonus based on a time allowance. One scheme was geared to the weight of output per man-hour.[16]

The American Brush industry was also an area where incentive payment schemes were used in most factories. Usually cash equivalents were determined for the standard times required to perform certain jobs. Commonly there was opportunity to earn extra pay of 20 to 33 percent by bettering the standard time allowance. In case an operative disputed the allowance for standard time or the evaluation of the job, the matter would be turned over to proper grievance committees with union representation.[17]

In sharp contrast to the companies producing furniture and electric motor gear, there was little evidence of incentive plans in over 20 plants associated with the Electricity Supply industry. Aside from a second minor instance, only one company could be said to have an incentive plan in operation. In this latter case the plan covered 90 percent of a work force amounting to 3,000. To determine the incentive bonuses, a committee representing management and union passed upon the evaluations by time study officers.[18]

Based on their observations the report by the British Trade Union Officials states that should unions, guided by the necessities of a given economic situation, elect to operate under an incentive plan with predetermined work loads, it behooves them to make certain that the work loads are fair and the incentive plans practical. Inefficient methods of operation should not be permitted to restrict earning opportunities. To make the proper checks, however, and to promote better methods of production, it was pointed out that unions must provide themselves with personnel trained in scientific management and production engineering.[19]

PIECE RATES

It was the belief of the British observers that American unions generally prefer high hourly rates to piecework, particularly in the industries which have been largely mechanized. Members of the productivity team studying the Valve industry were surprised to find that 8 of the 17 Valve companies visited in the United States had no piecework schemes in operation. Yet such methods are practically the general rule for the Valve industry in Britain. The report of the Valve team declared, however, that in the American companies where piece rates were in use, they were well received by the operatives.[20] The report of the specialist team on Welding noted that after prolonged research and an extensive period of actual trial the prevailing attitude of both unions and management in America is that piecework operation has serious inadequacies.[21]

Yet it was found that unions in certain industries, such as the Clothing trades, are not opposed to piece rates. For instance, in the Ladies' Garment Making industry the I. L. G. W. U. not only accepts piece rates, but also because of the small size of many firms and their highly competitive market, actually makes the time studies and determines the work standards which regulate the amount of output expected for particular rates.

The productivity report on the Men's Clothing industry cited several factors which make the piecework system attractive to operatives in this industry. It was noted that a great many of the workers have many years of experience in the Clothing trade. Accordingly the work previously processed has been accurately and skillfully handled and thus high output by the next operative is facilitated. Again, management keeps on the alert in this industry to assure the constant flow of work throughout the plant.[22] Another encouraging factor cited in this report is the realization by the workers in the Men's Clothing industry that piece rates, once scheduled, may not be changed except by agreement. Consequently, if a worker puts out more effort, there is nothing to prevent him from getting the proportionate increase in earnings.[23]

The British specialists in the Internal Combustion Engine industry learned that the majority of the plants visited paid on a piecework basis.[24] Members of the Cotton Yarn Doubling team reported that while both time and piece rates were found in the plants visited, most workers were on piece rates, especially in the Southern mills of this industry.[25] Moreover, British representatives of the Grey Ironfounding industry learned that American unions in this industry do not object to piecework methods nor to the amount of work each operative might wish to perform, as long as the rates are fair. One foundry was mentioned where operatives had agreed to accept a reduced rate in order to meet competition which had lowered the sales volume. Though the national union was officially on record against such an adjustment it did not act in this case, out of deference to the attitude of the union local.[26]

After examination of numerous union-management agreements in the Footwear industry, the British team specializing in this area concluded that the manufacturers decided for themselves the methods of wage payments and the amount in each case. While the unions did have a voice in these important issues, there was nothing to indicate that any joint agreement took place prior to the decision, or that there was any mutual understanding on the method of arriving at a given rate, or on the process of investigation.

This situation appeared authoritarian to the British productivity team on Footwear since in England it is the practice for both sides to work with boards of conciliation and arbitration and thus arrive at a schedule of piece rates by methods which are mutually acceptable. Nevertheless it was conceded by the British team that the end result for the American shoe worker may not appear objectionable to him; since if the pay check was large enough, the American shoe worker did not concern himself with the method of computing it.[27] In the case of the British Footwear industry the principle of joint consultation is so imbedded in the thinking of the workers that the entire piece rate structure for this industry depends upon a framework of national joint consultation, with local interpretation by boards of arbitration represented by employers and workers.

The British report on Footwear pointed out, moreover,

that the lack of any agreement between American management and unions on the method for fixing piece rates inevitably has led to an assortment of systems, which, though they may be satisfactory on a local scale, prevent the achievement of a national wage pattern based on a comprehensive understanding of the industry by leaders on both sides. A glaring instance of the confusion and duplication which has resulted in rate setting by encouragement of local patterns was the description of the piece rate structure in Brockton, Massachusetts, an area producing one-third of the shoe output in the United States. Here an independent union, the Brotherhood of Shoe and Allied Craftsmen, maintains 15 different craft locals under conditions of extreme competition and frequent jurisdictional controversy.

A reason given by the manufacturers for the high labor cost of the Brockton area, as compared to other shoe producing areas in the country, is this top heavy union structure built on an extremely complex pattern of piece rates. It is necessary to consult each of these 15 craft locals separately when determining rates. Furthermore, within each craft local there may be five gradings of skill with corresponding pay rates. In practice, some manufacturers have been known to pay third grade (or lower) piece rates to workers turning out first grade work, with operatives embittered as a result. Manufacturers as well become resentful upon learning that a competitor was conceded a lower grade piece rate on shoes selling at a higher price. The plight of the manufacturer in trying to estimate his selling price can be appreciated when it is realized that he must first negotiate with several separate craft locals.

A minor exception to the generally confused procedure

of rate setting in the shoe area was found in the case of the Industrial Union of Master Craftsmen. This small independent union of 850 members is allowed equal voice in setting piece rates with the manufacturers who recognize it. Only 8 wage brackets are observed by this union though internal adjustments based on skill are allowed. Adequate data on the financial and manufacturing operations of the companies are supplied to the union. Excellent relations exist between the employers and employees with the union acting as the intermediary.[28]

British observers believed that the chaotic pattern of piece rates in the Shoe industry, especially in Brockton, Massachusetts, is an exception to the prevailing situation in America. In other areas where piece rates are established by joint negotiation between unions and management, it is believed that companies are effectively prevented from reworking piece rates to meet the bid of the latest manufacturing contract. Instead, estimates for new production contracts are based on accepted piece rates previously agreed to by the unions. Management concentrates its efforts to better its competitive position by improving methods of production, not by shaving piece rates.[29]

Though individual incentive bonus plans were found to have considerable application, the members of the Non-Ferrous Metals team declared in their report that Americans tended to favor group coverage. In some cases they extended it to a department or to a whole plant. By contrast this same report noted that in the United Kingdom the general tendency is to gear piece rates to individual bonus schemes, because British workers object to having their earnings dependent on the output of other workers who may not be so efficient. The British visitors added that the answer of American unions to this objection is that trade union representatives make it their business to weed out workers who do not pull their load, since the aim is to keep earnings as high as possible. Any factor interfering with this goal, including "free riders," is marked for removal.[30]

Concluding its comments on piece rates, the British report on American Trade Unions and Productivity pointed out that most unions in the United States disapprove of piece rates in any form on the grounds that they are subterfuges for avoiding basic increases in wage rates for all operatives. The unions contend that every worker should share in the benefits of greater productivity even though the actual increase took place in only one department or section of a plant. Though this position of the unions yields a theoretical gain to the company for improved productivity during the life of an existing wage contract, the unions believe that the disadvantage is outweighed by greater loyalty of the members who have a common interest in the unified wage structure throughout the entire plant.[31]

GUARANTEED WAGES

The British team on Meat Packaging and Processing which visited the United States in 1950 was impressed by the operation of the guaranteed annual wage in one American packing plant, presumably the Hormel Company. The team members were told that under this plan an operative joining the work force in April of a given year will not be dismissed before the following April, save for violation of company rules or misdemeanor. They learned that this plan had been in continuous operation for 13 years. In comparison the team noted that most of this company's competitors provide for less than a week's notice in case of dismissal and it is the normal procedure to reduce the work force in the other firms of the industry during the slack period of the year.[32]

Further discussion on the Hormel guaranteed annual wage plan was presented in the appendix of the Meat Packaging report. There it was pointed out that, in agreement with the union and in accordance with the Fair Labor Standards Act, employees of the company may be engaged up to 53 hours per week without overtime pay unless 10 hours are exceeded in any one work day. In such case overtime begins after 48 hours in that week. The team report observed that all employees are paid on a weekly basis and are assured 52 weeks' notice before a lay-off. Actually the work weeks are heaviest in the winter and lightest in the summer. Thus the employees enjoy both a steady weekly income and a summer season with generous leisure time. To make the plan a success it was found that careful scheduling is necessary so that temporary workers are not required.[33]

PENSION PLANS

In addition to the features mentioned above in regard to pay systems, the British observers were impressed by the extensive use of pension plans throughout various American industries. Members of the team reporting on Food Canning noted that in the plants visited some pension schemes were fully financed by the employers, while other plans were based on joint contributions. Under this latter type employees earning up to $3,000 were required in a typical instance to put aside two percent of their wages and those earning over $3,000 four percent. It was acknowledged by the team members that the pension benefits were a little more generous than those received in Britain. Moreover, they are paid in addition to the security benefits under the Old Age Insurance Act.[34]

Members of the Cotton Yarn Doubling team found that most Southern mills maintain a noncontributory pension plan for their workers. Though all the employees are covered in most mills, one plant was found where retirement benefits were limited to executive, technical, and supervisory employees. Another plan, which was given rather thorough examination, permitted an employee with forty years of continuous service to retire at 65 with benefits, including social security, approximating one-half of his earnings just previous to retirement.[35]

It was considered noteworthy in the Productivity Team Report for the Pressed Metal industry that American labor has insisted on retirement benefits on a company basis despite the Federal Security program. The successful outcome for this demand in the case of the United Steelworkers was duly noted.[36] Under the Steelworkers' pension plan a worker on retirement receives a monthly benefit of one percent of his average monthly wage for the last ten years of employment multiplied by the number of years in service with the company. This monthly pension, however, at the time of the visit by the British Trade Union Officials, included the payment under Federal Old Age Insurance. Accordingly, the burden on the Steel companies was reduced as Federal Old Age Benefits increase. Hence, it is believed that Steel employers were instrumental in bringing about the substantial additions in Old Age Benefits recently granted by Congress.

The Steel companies argue that shifting more of the

burden to government is the only equitable way to meet pension requirements since the added cost is equalized for all companies and industries.[37] At the time of the report by the British Trade Union Officials in 1950 it was observed that a steelworker with monthly earnings of $400 and with 25 years of continuous service could receive a monthly pension of $100, including Federal Old Age Benefits.[38]

The team report on Meat Packaging and Processing stated that there are many contributory pension schemes among packing companies. The smaller packers arrange with an insurance company to credit the joint premiums to an annuity account for each employee. Ordinarily the prerequisite for a pension benefit is 20 years of steady and satisfactory employment with one company and retirement at 65 years of age for men and 60 years for women. Provision is made for the return of the worker's contribution should service be terminated before retirement.[39] The fact that pension benefits are not transferable, should an employee move to a different company, is regarded as a defect by the Steelworkers' union. The union expects to remove this drawback at a later date. On this point it was found that painters and electricians in New York City operate under a city wide pension agreement with their employers whereby the latter pay into the union pension fund two percent of their payrolls.[40]

WELFARE BENEFITS

In regard to welfare benefits contained in union-management contracts, members of the productivity team on Coal Mining were particularly impressed by the welfare, medical, and retirement fund established for the Coal industry in 1946. Yet the members of the productivity team did not consider that this plan, or that of any other welfare organization in American industry, was comparable to the Miners Welfare Commission in Britain. The British observers noted that the unity of purpose so outstanding in the field of production between workers and employers is only sporadic on problems relating to the general well being of miners. Further, the Coal report adds that until recent years the chief points of discussion stressed in negotiations by the United Mine Workers dealt only with wages, hours, and general working conditions.

Until 1946 in the Coal industry the miner was dependent upon the company doctor almost entirely. Furthermore, to attract doctors to such isolated areas as coal towns, before the present plan became effective, a certain rate of income had to be assured. This situation led to the general practice of prepayment by deducting from wages an average of $2.00 a month in 1946 for a married man with dependents. To provide for the advantage of hospital care an extra deduction of $2.00 was required. Under the present plan all such deductions are paid into the Mine Workers' Welfare Fund. This change in method of payment, however, had not yet greatly altered the contrast in hospital facilities as between large towns and cities with good public health care, and isolated mining towns where hospitals are inadequate or nonexistent.

Nevertheless, an historic advance was made in the social well being of American miners following the Krug-Lewis Agreement of 1946. Provision was made for a welfare and retirement fund supported by an assessment on the companies of 5 cents for every ton of coal mined. Three trustees were placed over the administration of the fund, one appointed by the United Mine Workers, one by the owners, and a third selected by the first two. The Medical and

Hospital Fund now maintained through pay deduction also is in the care of trustees who are appointed by the president of the Miners' union. Their exclusive province is to decide questions of eligibility, size of benefits, and the like. By 1951, the levy on coal tonnage had been graduated to the rate of 30 cents per ton. It is the intention of the Miners' union to discontinue pay deductions for medical and hospital service as soon as the fund for this purpose is actuarially secure.

Under the present contract a death benefit of $1,000 is paid to the widow or dependents upon the death of a miner. A disabled miner receives $60 per month, with additional grants of $20 for his wife and $10 for each child. A widow's benefit is $60 and $10 additional for each child. Orphaned children are allotted $25 per month. When mine workers attain the age of 60 and have accumulated 20 years of service in the Coal industry, they are eligible for pensions of $100 per month. As the pension plan now stands it is possible to leave the mining industry at 45 years of age and still claim the pension benefit at 60, as long as 20 years of service in the industry are to one's credit. Though acceptance of the pension payments bars a miner from further work in the Coal industry, no barrier is placed on acceptance of employment elsewhere. Unlike the case in other American industries, the pension of $100 per month cannot be reduced as benefits from the Federal Old Age Insurance System are increased.[41]

An important advance since the establishment of the Medical and Hospital fund has been the founding of 10 area medical offices, each supervised by a physician qualified in matters of organization and administration. A health program involving four stages is administered by the Medical officers: (1) Miners receiving disability or retirement benefits have available to them hospital service and rehabilitation care; (2) This same group of beneficiaries can also obtain home service and surgery, including medication duly prescribed by the physician; (3) Provision is being made for broadening of hospital and medical care to include all miners and their dependents; (4) Finally, it is intended to establish a general program of public health service and preventive medicine in conjunction with existing public health agencies to remove the abject living conditions still prevalent in many coal mining towns.

Medical care for miners in need of it is now on a systematic basis. The area medical officer decides on the qualifications of individual doctors, hospitals, and drug stores. Acceptability under medical standards and by the union members is a necessary requirement for physicians. Willingness to provide medical service at a reasonable charge is another stipulation. General practitioners and specialists who are willing to serve under these conditions are listed locally so that union members can be informed in advance of need for treatment. The medical fund does not defray the cost of dental and optical services unless such treatment is required to cure the illness covered by the fund.

The area medical offices have made extensive studies in the field of rehabilitation. By careful examination of old records many cases of bedridden miners were found who for 15 or 20 years had been unable to make progress against the handicap of broken backs, or amputated legs. The medical and hospital fund financed the transportation of such men by ambulance, special train, or plane to hospitals and clinics equipped for such cases and previously beyond the means of miners. A number of such men, once

considered in hopeless condition, are now earning a livelihood in new occupations. The hospitals as well have made
new advances in industrial rehabilitation from the study
of these cases.[42]

Unlike the position taken by management in the Steel
industry, the United Mine Workers insist that the burden
for their claims to pensions and other benefits should be
borne by the Coal industry itself. They oppose the shifting
of this cost to the Federal government by allowing coal
companies to lessen their payments for special security
benefits. The union emphasizes that the development of
the rehabilitation program for injured miners is of particular urgency for this industry because of the high ac-
cident rate in coal mining. Since the welfare and medical
funds have only recently been founded, the members of
the British productivity team on Coal did not feel qualified
to predict what the ultimate impact may be. Nevertheless,
it was believed the welfare programs had already en-
hanced the industrial status of the Coal industry. In regard
to health and welfare programs for American industry as a
whole, the team members stated that most of these measures have not yet achieved the standards prevailing in
Britain.

On the matter of state compensation for injuries and
industrial disease, the variation in the 48 state laws on this
subject prevented the team members from recognizing
any average standard. Here again, however, the Coal team
declared that in no case did they find compensation
schedules comparable to those in Britain. Particular weak-
nesses noted in the American laws were the limited time
periods for benefits even in the case of total disability. In
no case were payments continued after 10 years. Further,
in regard to industrial disease, only one such hazard has

recognition in the American Coal industry, silicosis. Yet at least one other disease, pneumoconiosis, is a basis for compensation in Britain.[43]

The British report on *Trade Unions and Productivity* called attention to the general lack of sickness and injury benefits found in the Federal Social Security program. It was noted that workers in America to obtain such protection make use of small industrial insurance policies, or carry insurance for this purpose sponsored by their trade unions. A number of union-company contracts now provide joint plans for sickness and disability insurance.[44] On this point members of the Electricity Supply team in their report remarked on the existence of mutual aid societies and sick benefit funds, usually sustained by joint contributions of public utility companies and their workers. These measures provide health services in addition to company facilities and are also supplementary to the services of the family physician.[45]

SUMMARY

Members of the British teams learned that American unions like to bargain with companies enjoying good profits since they connote efficiency, steady employment, and ability to pay higher wages. Little enthusiasm was encountered among American unions, however, for profit sharing plans. The preference here was decidedly in favor of increased regular wages. Incentive plans and piece rate systems were found to be less prevalent in America than in Britain. In a number of instances both management and unions regarded such plans as a source of discontent, and a cause of premature aging of workers. Yet where unions had opportunity to check on their performance, these systems in some companies were proving successful. Pension programs in private industry appeared to be more generous than is the case in Britain. Few of the plans though were computed on a basis independent from the grants under the Federal Social Security Act. The British productivity team on Coal Mining stressed the beneficial results already gained from the Miners' Welfare Plan jointly sponsored by management and the union in the American Coal industry.

CHAPTER SIX

Following Up the Team
Recommendations

During the summer of 1953, a visit to Britain made it possible to obtain at firsthand from former members of productivity teams and from other union and management representatives some appraisals on the effects in Britain of the team visits to America. Through the good offices of Sir Thomas Hutton, Director of the British Productivity Council, and Mr. T. A. Prichard, its Industrial Liaison Officer, management and union officials were interviewed in London, Manchester, the Midlands, and Scotland. Effort was made to determine the impact of team recommendations bearing on industrial relations in selected industries throughout Britain. Below are summaries of these interviews with representatives of unions and management in various sections of England and Scotland.

IRON AND STEEL

One of the first calls made in London by the writer was at the Iron and Steel Federation. There Mr. R. S. Keeling, Secretary of the Federation and also Secretary of the Iron and Steel productivity team, discussed some implications flowing from the Iron and Steel team visit to America. This team had suggested as recommendations that wage contracts be more highly systematized and that job evaluation studies might serve as a basis for determining payments.[1] The team suggested that attention be given to the shorter apprenticeships in the American Steel industry. Members of the team were impressed by the single union structure in the American Steel industry as against the many British craft unions.

With the report then in circulation for over one year, Keeling believed that it was regarded more as an occasion for fresh study of the Iron and Steel industry than as a definitive basis for such a study. Nevertheless, many in the British Steel industry now favor the American practice of job evaluation. Yet they are undecided whether it should be an immediate undertaking or be listed as a long term aim. Apparently the majority favor the long term approach on the basis that efforts to control the cost of living might be hampered should widespread re-evaluations of jobs take place immediately. There is apprehension that upward revision of wage rates might cause inflation.

The American visit did not result in precise conclusions on the question of incentive pay methods. It was obvious that incentive pay alone does not explain the greater output per man-hour in America, and that the cause of greater output in the United States is not found only in the workers themselves. Furthermore, attention was called to the fact that the use of individual and group incentive plans has been a long established practice in the British Steel industry.

A distinct advantage flowing from the Iron and Steel team's visit to America is a growing development of productivity consciousness in the industry. Since 1952, a productivity committee has been established made up of management and union representatives. Though some heavy unemployment has resulted in Wales from the installation in 1951 of continuous hot strip mills for producing tin plate, unions now regard such temporary dislocations as a necessary consequence from the use of new and better methods. Moreover, in the Welsh area the companies endeavored to keep more people on the payroll by arranging a guaranteed wage agreement of four days' pay per week. This short work week was not regarded as adequate by most workers. Over a longer period, it was considered in this industry that more mechanization means greater expansion and greater output. Meanwhile, an attempt is being made to keep the older and smaller companies in operation by assigning them special orders.

In contrast to the situation in the United States, the British Steel industry regards traditional craft unions as one of the biggest problems in industrial relations. Rigid adherence to obsolete work practices generally has not been overcome. One feature in common with a number of American unions was found in the strong insistence on the use of seniority by unions in the British Steel industry.

Another representative of this industry, Mr. J. P. Lowery of the Engineering & Allied Employers' National Federation, stated that greater impetus towards raising steel output followed from the Iron and Steel team report.

Commenting on a recommendation in the report that a simpler wage structure should be adopted, he observed that no satisfactory method has been devised as yet to change the wage structure fundamentally without considerable cost to management. Workers insist that no one shall suffer a loss. In effect this means that high bonus recipients might get even more wages. Company executives argue among themselves whether conversion to a simpler wage structure will really mean higher wages without greater output. Anticipating more severe cost competition in the future it is felt there is still no assurance that a simpler wage pattern will increase output. Lowery observed that there must be more thinking on the issue of the wage structure. In general the problem is apparent and a theoretical solution is known. However, the cost factor acts as a barrier.

In the British Steel industry Lowery saw no important opposition by workers to the use of piece rates. Group piece rate plans prevail to some extent, but there is a growing trend toward individual rates. On certain types of jobs naturally a difference of opinion arises in regard to method of application. Where the arrangement on piecework has been "mutually agreed on" between the company and the man, the union will not intervene. If a number of workers are involved, however, the shop steward may enter the picture. Piece rates have been used in British steel for fifty years.

Lowery noted that in the Diesel industry a recommendation was made to ban piecework; yet workers in general accept it. The aim should be to improve this method. Piece rate patterns as such are not of great national consideration, though they are of importance within districts. Between Steel districts, patterns vary quite widely. Though

piece rates are high generally, some districts have over a
long time paid at a low level, perhaps because of the type
of work.

One member association in the Engineering & Allied
Employers' Federation was so disturbed by the diversity
of piece rates in Britain that it set up a department of work
study to simplify them. Full time experts in work study
were assigned to give six weeks' courses in the subject for
management people. The unions welcome this approach.
One course is open to rate fixers and an appreciation
course is made available for higher management to enable
officials to examine new jobs so that they may be arranged
more scientifically.

In regard to job evaluation, Lowery noted that individual companies have been making use of it for many years,
especially the more efficient companies. The Iron and Steel
report has served to show the target for job evaluation
which should be considered by industry in general.

While on a national level it is hard to get general union
acceptance for work study in the factory, a fair success has
been achieved in this industry. Both union and management officials now see the value of such a study. Objec-
tions are becoming less frequent by top union officials
when, in the case of individual companies no complaints
have been heard and both the union local and the management agree to a job study project. The team report has
therefore promoted job evaluation. It is a natural development in Lowery's opinion.

In regard to the use of stop watch studies some representatives from both unions and management are inclined
to accept the method. Yet certain unions are opposed to
this device and have enforced strict rules against it since
the Bedaux days of rate cutting. Lowery believes that edu-

cation will help here by showing the benefits which can result to both company and worker. In a number of cases where the stop watch has been applied workers have readily appreciated its advantages.

Lowery considered that elastic rules are in effect on the question of apprenticeship. The Ministry of Labor has been requesting different industries to determine if a shorter training period might be introduced. Often there is a tendency to postpone making a decision because of the restraining bond of tradition. Yet with the longer span of education now, before entering the shop, some reduction in the length of apprentice training seems timely.

On the question of collective bargaining, the point was emphasized that negotiations already take place on the local level. Bargaining at the national level includes only the minimum safeguards, such as the national minimum wage, but not details. Rarely does the national association of Engineering Employers deal with individual piece rates. It is true that increases in wages are made nationally when based on the cost of living and greater national output. Nevertheless, there is today a wide range of wages based on plant considerations in regard to which the national association does not intervene. Such variations depend upon individual plant standards.

To determine the views of union representatives on some of the recommendations in the Iron and Steel team report, the comment of Mr. Jack Tanner, then President of the British Trades Union Congress is significant. Mr. Tanner served as a member of the Anglo-American Productivity Council. Similar to the position taken by Keeling of the Iron and Steel Federation, Tanner emphasized that the American model for industry will hardly serve as a definitive plan for reconstruction in Britain. It must be kept in mind that great stress is placed in England on special order products and quality lines. This situation is somewhat different from the concentration on mass production items throughout most of American industry. In any case, Tanner believed that British industry should make use of American methods wherever possible. He observed that many people in Britain accept readily enough the general argument for the need of greater output. Upon its application in their particular cases, however, they may tend to find reasons why change of methods or volume may not be appropriate at the present time.

With regard to the suggestion that the length of apprentice periods might be shortened, Tanner noted that the Ministry of Labor has urged that the apprenticeship period of 7 years should be reduced to 5. To encourage the more able youths to enter training, the Engineering Union has insisted that the apprentice should be paid a higher percentage of the skilled worker's wage.

Because of the present wage structure, Tanner pointed out that youngsters at ordinary work can earn more than apprentices. Even some machine tenders receive greater wages than do craftsmen. Yet Tanner found that companies thus far have not seen any great need for revamping the wage structure or training period for apprentices since, according to Tanner, there is an excess of applicants for apprentice training.

Actually, the wartime practice of giving full status to workers who had not completed a regular apprenticeship is now being discontinued. Even during the war such "dilutees," as they were called, had to register. While the unions wanted these men to be dropped when skilled men were available, management preferred to hold on to them as long as possible. In general Tanner saw no great urgency to relax present apprentice rules. He noted that while in the South of England there have been some verbal agreements to shorten the period of training, the full apprentice period is strictly observed in Scotland.

An element which Tanner regarded as bulking large in British industrial relations is the role of tradition. Besides its impact on apprenticeship, he noted that it has a strong influence in dissuading skilled men from moving to new job locations when change of residence is involved.

In the opinion of Mr. Hugh D. Byrne, Personnel Officer for Armstrong-Whitworth & Co., Ltd., Tynemouth, England, the productivity team reports have intensified action around Newcastle in favor of incentive plans to increase output. Both unions and management have studied the reports and obtained helpful ideas from them. On this point, it is important to have an appreciation of the industrial background in the Newcastle area. Some men now in the shops were once unemployed for a period of 14 to 20 years and thus had to live on charity. This experience has left them with a deep distrust of management and with a disposition to avoid exerting extra effort. Belief is strong that employment will be shortened by speeding up the job. Since those of the younger generation either remember the depression or have heard vivid accounts of it from their parents, they tend to reflect a similar attitude toward industry and management.

Another source of bitterness for workers around Newcastle goes back to the old school type of labor relations. In previous times the plant manager would arrogantly assert his authority over the work force and brook no discussion. Modern industrial relations still suffer a handicap from the memories of those days. It manifests itself in the worker's fear of wage cutting if greater effort is put forth.

Should a stop watch be introduced to time a job in the Newcastle area operatives would immediately walk out. Yet Byrne noted that in London workers readily accept the use of the stop watch in job study.

Strangely enough, in 1953 wages around Newcastle were still being computed on the 1914 basis by a series of war bonuses with no reality behind them. Both unions and management see the need for a new wage structure. The present antiquated arrangement of a long series of bonuses is regarded as a nuisance.

Byrne saw advantageous results in negotiating with unions for a shorter apprentice period. In contrast to Tanner's observations, Byrne found that the union will take the matter up with the work force and generally approves a reduction of apprentice time. He maintained that if a union is given the facts and a straight story it will approve a shorter training period in the vast majority of cases.

STEEL FOUNDING

Among the recommendations bearing on industrial relations made by the productivity team for this industry were the use of joint union-management production committees, more laborsaving machinery, and a simpler and fairer wage system.[2] One of the members of the Steel Founding team was Mr. W. L. Hardy, Foundry Manager of Lake & Elliot, Ltd., Braintree, England. It was his belief that operatives in American foundries do not work harder physically than foundrymen in Britain. Nevertheless, Americans produce a greater output because of a flair for job simplification and reduction of skill required in a number of work units. In addition there is the stimulus of a higher wage which accompanies simpler job functions.

By way of comparison Hardy observed that it is rather difficult to institute work changes in Britain. Men are suspicious about retiming jobs. He believed that too much regard is held for tradition. The conservative attitude of the British craftsmen tends to hold back progress. In America he noticed that workers quickly cast aside old methods if they are considered overly time consuming.

The postwar attitude of relaxation in Britain on the assumption that the worst is over has also been a retarding factor. Moreover, Hardy added that up to the present little hope for increased wages through extra effort has been possible for British workers. The frequent question they ask about new machinery or new methods is how such changes will benefit them. Until substantial proof is forthcoming that British workers will share an extra material advantage, Hardy does not look for outstanding success from the new methods. Yet he believed if workers are allowed to earn all they can, they will give what is wanted of them and their suspicion will diminish. Similarly if they are sure of a higher standard of living they will co-operate in the use of new equipment. On this point Hardy noted that while wages are about the same in value as before the war, dividends have gone up sharply. He considered that better results might have been forthcoming if workers had shared to a greater extent in these corporate earnings.

Hardy emphasized that a number of British union officials have vigorously campaigned for greater output. This policy requires courage because elections to union office may be lost as a result of it. In general Hardy considered that British unions are less receptive to new methods than are American unions.

An interim report in 1952 by the A. A. C. P., based on information obtained from 19 Steel Founding firms, revealed that the American visit had a sharp impact on the British industry. Three Productivity conventions have been held by the British Steel Foundry Association since the publication of the team's report and a permanent productivity committee is in operation. Meetings and discussions on American practices are still being held.[3]

Little progress has yet been made though in simplifying the wage structure in this industry. For the present the incentive to earn more income has been provided by the necessity of coping with the sharp increase in living costs since 1949.[4] There still seems to be difficulty in persuading British workers that earnings should be related to the amount of work done. Professor P. Sargent Florence of the University of Birmingham believes that British workmen are satisfied with too modest a standard of living.[5] Moreover, they are inclined to see a reduction in profits rather than an increase in output as the way to obtain wage increases when necessary. Florence is of the view that little heed is given to the point that at least half of a firm's profits must be expended for new equipment.[6] At the 1952 Productivity conference for Steel Founding, strong exception was taken by some of the participants to the position of Florence that British workers are not interested in bettering their standard of living.[7]

Florence himself has declared that the chief responsibility for social progress, steady employment and a better standard of living will have to be borne by top management of the big companies. The more enterprising and efficient executives must be placed in the key positions if this responsibility is to be met.[8] Until men with broader vision exert more influence it is not likely that capital expenditure for mechanical equipment will be increased adequately. At present it is estimated that mechanical horsepower available at the elbow of a British worker averages about 3 units; in America, the average is 8 or 9.[9]

STEEL CONSTRUCTION

The productivity team for this industry suggested in its report that attention might be given to the advantages in a single union structure which greatly lessens problems of jurisdiction. The team members were impressed by the readiness of American union representatives on the local level to work along with management in the adoption of new methods of production. It was recommended that British union officials take courses in work study programs so that less friction would develop in putting them in practice. The suggestion was also made that unions might show greater willingness to allow workers who have served no apprenticeship to accept promotions in rating.[10]

To gauge the effect of such recommendations, the comments of the leader of the productivity team on Steel Construction, Mr. Harold B. Denton, Chairman of Joseph Parks & Sons, Ltd., Cheshire, are noteworthy. His observations were made about a year after the team's report had been circulated through the industry. Denton pointed out that in assigning work to men in Britain a recognized pattern, centuries old, must be observed. Craft organizations, which have been part of British industry from the Middle Ages, still adhere to strong ties of tradition. For example, it is against custom to let a laborer use a wrench. If a man has served no apprenticeship he must remain in the unskilled class. Moreover, objection is even made to relaxation of rules so that older workers may undergo a training period. On the subject of special training programs on new methods Denton saw no evidence that unions were conducting them in his industry. He found no great reluctance, however, on the part of workers to adjust to the increase of mechanization. Denton observed that while in general there is an insufficient number of workers to serve the many projects planned since the end of the war, some companies are holding on to surplus men because of the heavy investment in their training.

For a time there was a joint consultation committee in the Joseph Parks Co. and the workers who participated were co-operative. Yet when they returned to the shop floor after each session, the question put to them was, "What have you got for us?" The rank and file only saw joint consultation in terms of something for them. Nevertheless, it was Denton's view that better human relations now exist in British industry because trade unionists from top to bottom are aware of the economic situation facing the country and believe that management is not out to exploit them.

DIESEL LOCOMOTIVES

Among the suggestions made by the team representing this industry was stress on the advantage of American work methods in that they are basically simplified to the extent of making many craft trades and apprenticeships unnecessary. The American type of industrial union was viewed with favor on the ground that it might remove many jurisdictional disputes. Advantage was seen in the use of higher hourly rates based on time studies as against the piece rate system. The team believed that greater effort should be taken to select men from the shop floor for supervisory positions.[11]

As a "follow-up" on these recommendations, comments are taken from an interview with Mr. L. G. Copestake, Technical Assistant to the Chief Designer of the North British Locomotive Co. Ltd., Glasgow, and a member of the Productivity team on Diesel Locomotives. He was impressed by the way the long apprentice period has been reduced in America. Instead of tediously waiting for more skilled men to be trained, as British companies are doing, both American management and unions have agreed to break down the jobs into simpler tasks. As a result there are fewer shortages among skilled men in America than is the case in Britain. Copestake found that foremen alone are required to have the all-round skills. He recalled that at the Blackpool Conference in England during 1951, changes were recommended for the apprentice system so that a greater number of able men could be utilized more effectively. The conference did not accept the recommendation, though it favored more extensive use to be made of semiskilled men.

Turning to the possibility of raising worker income in Britain, Copestake declared greater earning power must come through modernization of plants similar to what has already been done in America. There he found that material is put in and put out far more rapidly than in the United Kingdom. In this connection British workers will have to show more readiness to accept new methods. He acknowledged that an error in policy by British management in the past was to introduce changes in methods without sharing any of the gains with the workers. It was pointed out that British companies are now going more into details when explaining changes to the men on the shop floor. Unions in turn are conducting courses for shop stewards. Yet on the whole Copestake believed enough has not yet been done on the explanatory side.

Another member of the Diesel team interviewed at this same company was Mr. R. R. Alexander, who was a union representative with the team. As an indication that action had been taken on the suggestion in regard to promotion from the shop floor, it should be pointed out that since the team visit Alexander had been promoted from electric welder to foreman. It was his belief that fear of unemployment is becoming manifest again with the growing competition from West Germany and Japan in the production of locomotives and ships. One effect is that workers are not putting out as much as before the war. Alexander recalled that welders in America get more done in a day than is the case with British workers. The old practice of spreading the work may be a factor. While full employment prevailed in the casting industry and in stove manufacturing, he made the observation that moulders in Glasgow were working on a four day week.

Other influences which have a retarding effect on worker output were mentioned. For example, wage rates vary widely. Alexander observed that some companies pay their welders twenty pounds per week ($56.00), while others pay as low as eleven pounds ($30.80). Poor layout of plants in Britain was also listed in this connection. While dirt floors in American factories were rarely encountered, they are by no means uncommon in the United Kingdom. The waning of natural resources in Britain now causes workers to look upon Canada as their hope. Its vast natural riches make a strong appeal to potential emigrants.

At the Blackpool conference, March, 1951, in which the

Diesel Locomotive Industry participated, limited acceptance was given the recommendation of the Diesel report that sweeping changes be made in the system of payment for craftsmen. Members at the Conference felt that the industry's products would have to be standardized to a much greater degree, and inefficiences in men and machines remedied, before the piece rate system could be replaced by higher hourly rates. Acknowledgment was made that the present piecework system has defects. It was agreed that improvement might be made through the use of a basic hourly rate with an over-all group bonus.[12]

BUILDING INDUSTRY

With the thought of possible adaptation in Britain, the Building team called attention in its report to the wide range in the permissible age of entry into apprenticeship for crafts in the American Building industry. Applicants are accepted usually between the ages of 17 and 25. Moreover, while the actual length of apprenticeship varied, the average period in America was found to be under four years. The need to develop more initiative and receptivity to new methods among British workers in the Building industry was emphasized.[13]

Comment on some of these observations was made by Mr. C. Gordon Rowlands, Secretary of the National Federation of Building Trades Employers and also secretary of the productivity team on Building. Rowlands pointed out that several attempts to improve the manpower situation in this industry had preceded the team's visit to America. As one instance, effort was made to shorten the apprentice period and place more boys in training. For some time there has been in existence a Joint Apprentice and Training Council to handle the growing number of apprentices.

Yet little progress has been made on reducing the period of apprenticeship. While management and unions have discussed this issue, most representatives of both groups are opposed to it, especially the older workers. Rowlands remarked, however, that extraordinarily good results have followed from the use of incentive plans by well organized firms with able management and supervisory staff. Such firms know how to apply incentive methods. In regard to the smaller building contractors, the incentive type of compensation appears to be a nuisance.

With respect to new methods of construction, it was noted that British workers tend to be slow to change their ideas. Nevertheless, there have been very successful exhibitions throughout Britain to promote new methods and equipment for the Building industry. The question remains as to how purchases of such equipment can be financed.

Rowlands emphasized that the lean war and postwar diet has slowed up the British worker. For example, a bricklayer before the war would lay more brick than is the case in 1953. In 1939, however, the diet of the average bricklayer was generous enough to allow him bacon and eggs for breakfast, a ham or cheese sandwich for a morning snack, and a good lunch besides. Such ample nourishment was not prevalent in 1953.

Another factor mentioned as partial explanation for the lowered efficiency of building operatives was the reduced general standard of living throughout the war years. It is now apparent to British workers that they are at least getting along better than during hostilities so there seems no great need to push to the last ounce. The constant cry of "wolf" in regard to a potential economic crisis leaves many workers unimpressed. Moreover, hope of a tangible increase in wage outlay from greater effort was still remote in 1953.

ELECTRIC POWER INDUSTRY

In the team report for this industry attention was called to the need of giving more care to the introduction of a man to his job by job instruction training. Advantage was found in the American system of progressive wage increases as a reward for greater skill on a job. The team members stressed the importance of training supervisors in the area of industrial relations.[14]

One of the members of the Electric Power team was Mr. R. G. Cook, National Industrial Officer for the Union of General and Municipal Workers. While in the United States, Cook came to the conclusion that American management is far more alert in regard to industrial relations than is the average British executive. He noted that there are some British managing directors who cannot even recall offhand the names of the managers in their various plants. The chasm between many British "top" executives and their workers is of course even wider. British management cannot assume that half of the men in the shop are on speaking terms with them as is frequently the case in America.

Cook noted that the mere fact an individual is the son of somebody important means much in British industry. By comparison at least, such a connection accounts for little in America. In effect the different attitude in the United States permits greater opportunity for men on the shop floor to move upwards.

On questions of industrial relations, Cook pointed out

that many boards of directors in the United States have vice presidents who are daily responsible for handling problems in this area. A similar situation is not true in Britain. With the exception of the nationalized industries and some of the bigger companies like Ford's, Cook believes there is nothing comparable in Britain to the typical industrial relations department of an American corporation with its high degree of autonomy.

In Cook's estimation, an industrial relations official should occupy a position midway between the worker and the director of operations. A worker should be able to go to such an official with a grievance and speak very frankly, with the feeling that he will get an unbiased hearing. It was Cook's opinion that few opportunities of this nature are found in Britain. From his own experience as a union official, he preferred to take a grievance matter directly to the plant manager instead of the personnel man. The latter would find too many reasons why the worker's appeal should be dropped. In effect Cook regarded most officials in British plants who handle labor relations as mere legs of executive management. Workers have no confidence in them.

It was Cook's view that industrial relations departments should be set up in a way that will permit easy communication. He maintained there should be a separation of function so that certain officials should deal exclusively with wages and working conditions. Other members of the staff might handle matters pertaining to health, athletics, and welfare. Cook remarked that if in the morning one argues bitterly with a man on wages, it is hard in the afternoon to talk with him on "general interest" problems.

In the opinion of this union official the nationalized industries in Britain are setting an encouraging pace toward better industrial relations. Generally the standard in the field is improving throughout Britain. The recent war helped to bring a more enlightened view. There is not so much tendency now to look upon industrial relations as just another costly department. Even with the most rugged managements, it is possible to discuss the problems at issue.

In regard to employee education, Cook was impressed by the desire of American management to let foremen know the trend of company policy. Good industrial relations cannot be established without this prerequisite. He noted that considerable progress in employee education has also been made in Britain. In the Electric Power industry, 25 percent of the staff of 40,000 have a good opportunity to attend schools sponsored by joint technical committees. Every year two sessions of six weeks' duration are held at Oxford and Cambridge. Two hundred students attend each time. Every effort is being made to make the Electric Power industry self-sufficient in respect to management and personnel.

A management representative on the Electric Power team was Mr. R. D. V. Roberts, Secretary of the National Joint Advisory Council of the British Electricity Authority. In his estimation the Electric Power industry now realizes the importance of properly introducing a man to his job. To this end indoctrination courses of four weeks' duration have been devised and are gradually growing. While supervisors are necessarily skilled craftsmen, there is still need to train them in various aspects of human relations. Accordingly two country establishments have been set aside where courses are conducted for supervisors all year round on several subjects which include joint consultation and human relations.

Concerning job evaluation there has been no development in this industry similar to the trend in America. While
negotiations always stress the evaluation of jobs, no use is
made of job classifications based on a specific point system.
Roberts considered it difficult to put into effect such a
method in Britain. He noted that an American team recommendation for the British Electric Power industry
pointed out the need for greater wage differentials between the skilled and the less skilled. A recommendation
in Roberts' team report for shorter apprenticeships and an
extension of the age limit at entrance has received no
action. Unfortunately a long history to the contrary stands
in the way of such changes.

PRINTING INDUSTRY

Among the recommendations contained in the two reports on the Printing industry was a suggestion that a more
realistic attitude be taken by both unions and management
to the long range economic situation facing this industry.
It was urged that more use be made of semiskilled workers,
that jurisdictional disputes be lessened, and that greater
receptiveness be given to new methods of production by
both unions and management. Training of new workers in
technical schools was encouraged. Team members stressed
that benefits from increased productivity should be shared
between employers and workers.[15]

Commenting on some of these recommendations, Mr.
L. E. Kenyon of the British Federation of Master Printers
stated that while major results are not yet apparent, the
men in the shops and union officials are now more productivity minded. Mr. Charles Birchall, leader of the team

on Lithographic Printing, has improved methods used in his plant at Liverpool. Stanley Gilman, who was a union representative on the team, has exerted a constructive influence when on speaking tours with Birchall. Printing trade union leaders now see greater output as the only salvation for themselves, for union members, and for the country. It took years to get them around to this point of view and the team reports were a major factor in the conversion. At present, officials in the Trades Union Congress are making efforts to get more union members aware of the need for greater output. The crucial problem concerns the attitude of union men on the shop floor and of many companies as well. The average employer still wants to keep working in the old way.

With respect to the greater use of semiskilled men, little progress has been made since vested union interests are against it. Recently, however, a number of men have been upgraded and older applicants have been accepted for training. Yet the area of expansion here is closely limited by worker attitudes, especially by craftsmen who have served an apprenticeship of seven years. There is still a deep fear that unemployment as it prevailed in the 1930's may return. The unions, moreover, feel that acceptance of newer methods must depend on assurance that the operatives will realize tangible benefits from them. Thus far there has not been too ready credence given to such promises. This attitude is one of the factors holding back the use of the double work shift. However, shortage of manpower also enters here.

In the opinion of Kenyon, demarcation or job jurisdiction is more of a problem in London than in the rural areas. London has a longer history of full size job organizations. When unemployment threatens there is a tendency to spread the work. It will be hard to overcome this tradition.

Kenyon pointed out that upwards of forty firms have adopted incentive payment plans since the team reports were published. Throughout 1952 a committee has been working on this problem. No flat recommendation was made since all parties concerned do not feel an advantage will be forthcoming.

It was noted by Kenyon that a great number of technical schools for printing are maintained in Britain and have excellent equipment, especially in London. Workers see modern printing devices in such schools and put pressure on companies to get similar machines. Industrial demand for new equipment has thus been stimulated. Ironically the strong competition in this industry coming from Holland in the past four years was built up by British machine companies who were ordered by the Government to develop foreign markets even if the home printing industry had to get along on reconditioned equipment.

According to P. J. Kilpatrick, Director, T. & A. Constable, Ltd., Edinburgh and a member of the team on Letterpress Printing, men from the shop floor were highly impressed in regard to speeds in American printing plants. Frequent meetings on the team report, after returning from the States, have promoted better understanding between employers and workers. Attention was called to the fact that unions have been recognized in this industry for a hundred years and that British Printing is now 98.9 percent organized.

Kilpatrick showed considerable enthusiasm for an incentive plan for presses, involving about twenty printing companies, which had been put in effect two weeks before the Letterpress Printing team came to America in 1950. An encouraging increase in output has been the result.

With respect to wages the Printing companies are aware that higher prices mean higher wage demands. However, since 1949 a five year period of stabilization has been in effect. While during this time there have been no changes in working conditions, adjustments in wages have been made in accordance with the cost of living index which increased from 114 to 140 since 1949. For each point over 114 wage increases were allowed by the Government.

Kilpatrick looked askance at the high wages demanded by American workers and noted that British operatives are more complacent on this point. Costly expenditures are rare for wage earners in the United Kingdom. Since distances are short, there is no great demand for cars, as contrasted with workers in America. The garden, which involves little expense, is the great psychological outlet in Britain. In general, the British see no advantage in "showing off" by trying to "keep up with the Jones." This psychological difference is partly reflected in the enormous divergence of wage levels between the British and American Printing industry. For example, Kilpatrick noted that compositors in the United States received at the time of his visit over $100.00 per week. Their British counterparts were then earning something over $20.00 per week.

Skepticism was expressed by Kilpatrick on whether union officials are convinced of an advantage in a shorter period of apprenticeship. He doubted also if management were convinced on this point. At present though the training period is officially six years, in practice it is five. National military service permits an allowance of one year. Kilpatrick considered that the great need in British industry is larger capital investment.

It is significant to compare Kilpatrick's management view on wages with that of Mr. W. P. McGinniss of Glasgow, District Secretary for the General and Municipal Workers' Union. In effect McGinniss stated that semiskilled and skilled machine workers in Scotland are content if they have a steady job and a good wage. They are not impressed with the high wages received in America even though a better living standard is the result. A number of items which make up the high living standard in America have little appeal for the Scotch. For instance, it was mentioned that the average worker sees a car as only an unnecessary burden. Moreover, his wife finds little attraction in the many household gadgets typical of American homes. As one reason for skepticism in regard to high wages in America, McGinniss recounted the case of a young man in the General and Municipal Workers' Union who went to New York with his wife and two sons to take a job as an elevator operator at $70.00 per week. Before long his wife had to go to work also in order to help pay living expenses. McGinniss failed to see much advantage in such high wages.

On the question of incentive plans, McGinniss believed there was no serious objection to them by Scottish workers. As long as more wages are received for greater output, the men are satisfied. He saw no difficulty in getting worker acceptance for new methods, new layouts, even time and motion studies, since they eventually mean greater output and higher wages. McGinnis emphasized that incentive schemes were well known in Scotland before the reports of the productivity teams. Courses on such methods have been taught for some years. Scientific management was also advocated in Scotland before the productivity teams. Both unions and management through a joint board endeavor to promote this approach to industry.

In the progress report for the Printing industry, based on data received from 26 companies, note is made that members of both the Letterpress team and the Lithographic team have each addressed over 100 meetings throughout the principal cities of Britain. Trade Union Officials have participated in a number of these sessions.[16] This progress report emphasizes that impressive results should not be expected from greater use of incentive schemes if they are merely added to obsolete production methods. Attention was called to the fact that where incentive schemes have been recently put into effect, they have been accompanied by a broad review of production techniques.[17]

Fear of unemployment is the factor which makes unions in the Printing industry hesitate to accept the recommendations for freer intake of workers, relaxation of jurisdictional lines, and the use of a double shift. One union official declared that more than a century of insecurity makes workers reluctant to take any action which might prejudice the present degree of security in the Printing industry.

Nevertheless in 1950 and 1951, a number of union and management agreements were reached for special increases of apprentices in most craft areas, besides the normal intake to overcome the post war shortage of labor. Further, the stipulation was made that some of these extra apprentices could be as old as 23, if they had been in military service. The usual top age limit for apprentices is 18. Some increase in double day shifts has developed but it is not extensive. It is the view of employers that the unions exaggerate the fear of unemployment.

An approach has been made by unions to the possibility

of amalgamation as a means to overcome complex lines of jurisdiction and to meet recent technological developments. It is not expected, however, that any immediate changes of a broad nature will develop since many unions are intent on preserving the present status of skilled craftsmen.[18]

BAKERY INDUSTRY

Members of the productivity team for this industry were impressed by the use of the double day shift in American bakeries. Their report also stressed the two way channels of information which exist between unions and management. The strategic importance of the foreman in presenting management policy was noted.[19]

One of the team members from this industry who visited America was Miss Alice B. Horan, Secretary of the Joint Industrial Council of the Cakes and Biscuits Industry and a National Officer of the General and Municipal Workers' Union. Miss Horan observed that at the beginning employers in the Cakes and Biscuits industry showed little interest in visiting America. Later they became enthusiastic about the project. In 1952, after returning to Britain, the companies through their Cakes and Biscuits association set aside a period of seven days to discuss the work of the team. Conferences were held with representatives from production, the employer association, and the unions. Papers were presented in seminars to emphasize the factors of chief value observed in America. One seminar was devoted to industrial relations. This arrangement permitted opportunity for employers to talk to the people who had made the recommendations in the team report.

At these sessions the employers showed readiness to approve the findings of the team.

In the opinion of Miss Horan, companies in the Cakes and Biscuits industry which recognize unions are more co-operative than others. Attention was called to the fact that one company which deals with no union and which is particularly isolationist in its approach to problems of the industry, is owned by Canadian and American capital. It was stated that this "American" company holds to the view that if there happens to be a union member in a Cakes and Biscuits firm, it is the fault of the employer. In other words, the way to keep unions out of a plant is to improve working conditions and thus remove any argument for a union. Miss Horan observed that opposition to unions is not typical of British companies.

Following the visit to America by the Cakes and Biscuits productivity team, some companies have instituted the use of double day shifts instead of operating on a day and night basis. The unions have not opposed this change. Sweeping modifications have not necessarily resulted from the American visit, but more improvements have been encouraged. There is an encouraging trend in providing the employer side with day to day information on industrial relations by the use of biweekly meetings with workers. More discussion is being given to time and motion study with special attention on its history and application to unions. The union attitude is favorable towards it if local union representatives are consulted beforehand. When such an arrangement is worked out, top union officials will not interfere.

From conferences with employers, following issuance of the team report on the Cakes and Biscuits industry, union members have gained knowledge and confidence about motion study. They now regard it as necessary and instead of the old fear about working oneself out of a job, the belief prevails that greater output and higher skill will be the ultimate outcome. Actually, the union in this industry claims partial credit for the more enlightened attitude of the workers on motion study. As early as 1951 Miss Horan's union realized that meetings and exhortations would not be enough to prepare the workers for new methods. In that year the union instituted a month's full time course on industrial relations for shop stewards and other men from the shop floor. For each member in the course the union paid a month's wages and expenses. A union congress held some time after this special course on industrial relations gave high praise to the benefits flowing from it.

In 1953, renewed effort was made by the General and Municipal Workers' Union to reach the men on the shop floor. It is now hoped that when production changes are inaugurated in a plant, the workers will not panic. Union leadership has already been prepared to meet the adjustments and can thus instill confidence in thousands of others. This slower and more painstaking approach is regarded as the only effective method and far superior to the emotional appeal of a mass meeting.

On the subject of unemployment Miss Horan pointed out that the fear of unemployment has not disappeared despite current high demand for workers. Memories of the dole, which was experienced by the majority of British workers in the 1920's, still persist and even color the thinking of young men in the shop who have heard stories of the great depression from their parents. From such a source youngsters can vividly describe the harshness of the now discarded means test, once used for unemployment relief. Under such a test parents had to prove that no income from any of their children living at home was available to support them. To escape the humiliation of a father living on his daughter's income it was not uncommon to persuade children to leave home.

Miss Horan noted that beginning under the Labor government, one method used to overcome fear of unemployment has been the construction of "industrial estates." Under this plan areas adjoining various cities and towns in England have been set aside for the development of diversified industries so that in the future whole towns or regions will not suffer severe unemployment because of a slump in one industry. It was the opinion of Miss Horan that maintenance of optimism coming from full employment will determine the success of the productivity teams. She recalled that the moderate textile recession of 1952 showed plainly that the old dread of unemployment can quickly be aroused.

COTTON TEXTILE INDUSTRY

Both the Cotton Spinning and the Cotton Weaving branches of this industry sent productivity teams to America. Of the several recommendations on industrial relations in the Cotton Spinning report, particular emphasis was placed on the need for workers and management to adopt new methods of operation and to accept work study programs. Attention was called to the necessity of changing work loads when improved work planning justifies it.[20]

A management member of the Cotton Spinning team and also its leader, was Mr. C. Henniker Heaton, Director of the Federation of Master Cotton Spinners' Association in Manchester. It was his belief that this team's report was very well received because of its spirit and factual presentation. Upon their return members of the team went into the cotton towns around Manchester and held meetings on the report. The questions and answers which resulted were later published. A snag developed, however, on the matter of work study. The Central Union Authority did not approve work study in principle. Fear was expressed about the circumstances surrounding the use of the stop watch. There is apprehension that fewer men will be employed should work study be instituted. Heaton acknowledged that a smaller labor force with better pay is one of the objectives.

Actually, local unions regard the present wage level as belonging to the prewar stage of mechanization. A change in wage structure must come. Older age workers tend to predominate in this industry though the number of employees has contracted in the past thirty years. A major reduction took place in the 1930's.

Union members of the old school find it hard to accept the new situation on work methods. Even so, attitudes vary with areas. Some union secretaries definitely approve work study and even take courses on the subject sponsored by the Cotton Board Authority. The Cotton Board is a development by the whole industry and has both employer and union representatives. Younger union men are also being trained in work study. The trend is now in the right direction.

In general Heaton believed that though some in management have been cool to work study, there has been an increased use of it since 1948 and much more so in 1953. The team report has speeded up the trend. Yet it is recognized that the American scene cannot be regarded as a key pattern for the British Cotton Spinning industry.

Mr. G. H. Jolly, also a member of this team, and a Special

Officer for the Cotton Spinners' Federation, is an expert on the subject of work study. Since his return from America he has been explaining new methods directly to operatives in the Lancashire area. Talks and question periods in the mills have helped to reveal opinions in regard to changes. Now younger people realize that higher output is an opportunity to raise their standard of living. Jolly stated that unions which are participating in work study do not approach the 100 percent mark in co-operation. He regarded both management and unions as slow in adopting it. In his estimation much depends on how operatives were treated by management in the past. In great part management will have to initiate the new methods and the workers will have to trust management meanwhile.

Among some additional recommendations made by the Cotton Weaving team were suggestions that greater attention be given to training workers so that maximum results would follow the adaptation of new methods. In regard to wage payments, it was proposed that a base rate and bonus plan be put into effect.

Speaking as Director of the Cotton Spinners' and Cotton Weaving Manufacturers' Association, Mr. D. B. Fielding noted that a piece rate plan has prevailed in Cotton Weaving for many years. However, he believed that it has anomalies and is unscientific. A Government commission in recent years examined the wage structure and recommended a better method of wage payment and the use of work study. The unions are now cooperating in devising an improved wage plan. Progress is being made though it is hard to change a wage system when certain groups of workers regard their higher pay rates as an inviolable right. Yet job evaluation shows some of them to be out of line with other wage rates.

Motion study trials have indicated that there is not much

opportunity here for work simplification. Fortunately, better types of machinery have helped by reducing physical work while increasing total output. Trips to America, even before the visit of the productivity team on Cotton Weaving, have shown that there are striking differences between British and American methods. One cannot often compare like with like in the two countries. Fielding stressed that the main thing is to be aware of the development already taking place in Lancashire. The industry is fully alive to the need for greater output. Yet there will not be violent, sudden changes. Attitudes of workers to new methods must be revised and this phase has largely been completed. Already better methods are being applied.

Concentration on war production was a big blow to the Cotton Weaving industry. Forty percent of the mills were closed by Government order. To resume operations after the war was a titanic task. Any purchase of new machinery required a license. A high purchase price and a tax also had to be met. Revision of the wage structure has now corrected many inequities. Motion study is making good progress with the aid of special courses conducted by the Cotton Board.

MEN's CLOTHING INDUSTRY

The recommendations in the report of the team representing this industry dwelt on the urgency of arranging work methods so that full use could be made of the skill possessed by each operative. Incentive systems, including straight piece rates, were considered a direct means of achieving higher output. The team acknowledged that workers must have confidence that rates will not be reduced with greater output. Full co-ordination between unions and management was considered a prerequisite to the achievement of maximum productivity.[21]

Noting that the team report recommended changes in work methods, Mr. M. K. Reid of the Wholesale Clothing Manufacturers' Federation pointed out that small companies have found it difficult to make substantial adjustments. Yet there has been considerable action taken by the big companies. A growing tendency is evident in the use of scientific management and better work planning. In general Reid believed there has been a noticeable improvement in the Clothing industry since the team report, substantiated by the greater production.

While unions in this industry are as desirous as the companies to obtain larger output, the former are suspicious of time and motion analysis. The union preference is for motion study as such. They fear that the time element is overstressed and suspect that outsiders who would reorganize a plant might cut wages as a result. Reid believes that if joint consultation of union and management is held in advance to remove suspicion, union co-operation will be forthcoming.

With respect to method of compensation, it appears that the unions are not enthusiastic about piece rates. Instead the preference seems to be for incentive bonus plans. A large percentage of workers in the Clothing industry is now on the incentive basis. Reid was of the opinion that the team report indicated that the American worker had a very different attitude toward the job from his British counterpart. The American seems to work harder for forty hours in order to earn the maximum. While British workers are not lazy, they prefer to set a quota of so many pounds a week and hold to it. Reid considered that there were many dis-incentives in the British economy. Old qualms are still in the workers' minds; they are fearful of using up the job. Recognition of the need for management to educate workers to the new methods was emphasized and progress is already being made in this direction.

Long before the Clothing team report, union-management relations in this industry were being carried on under a highly satisfactory organizational pattern. Constructive industrial relations have existed since 1911. In 1920 the first national agreement was put into effect. Local factory relationships are also considered good. Joint union-management councils for all sections of the industry are a major function today. At these sessions methods are promoted to increase productivity, efficiency and quality. The Joint Clothing Council, which is the successor to the Development Council set up by the Labor government, is receiving strong support from employers.

The Council has a technical staff to advise individual companies. It sends people to the factory floor to diagnose and make recommendations. This service is especially helpful for the smaller companies. The Council provides general information, conducts courses, makes surveys for industry, and issues reports. All these projects are carried on with a view to greater efficiency. While of course these activities are not directly an outcome of the productivity team reports, increased action has been stimulated by them. What did emerge from the team reports was therefore most beneficial, especially the importance of placing more stress on greater output. Much useful technical information was also made available to British companies.

A member of the team on the Men's Clothing industry, Mr. E. B. Walters, Director, Clifford Williams & Sons, Birmingham, declared that since the team's visit to America, thirty different types of machinery have been installed in his plant. Both workers and management share in promoting improvements. Greater use of mechanization, though it brought about job transfers, did not cause a cut in employment. Moreover, the average wage has increased.

This employer pointed out that while no union was recognized in his plant, the employees, who are 95 percent female, have pension, profit sharing, and health plans. Benefits for sick pay amount to one-half the average wage. Practically all of the work is done on a co-operative piece-work basis. A bonus system is set so that the average worker can earn the quota which is two-thirds of the average output. A type of joint consultation in regard to production is maintained. Walters stated that there was a turnover of only five percent in the plant. Moroever, many married women workers return in later life, after raising their children. All the executive staff in the company are now giving much attention to motion study. A few ideas on this subject are proposed by the workers themselves.

In regard to the Clothing industry generally Walters recalled that upon the return of the productivity team from America, lectures were held throughout the industry. In his opinion the outstanding benefit from the visit to the United States was the deeper realization of the need for greater output. More awareness has developed in regard to the benefits of specialization. A stronger inclination to use piece rates is evident either on a group or individual basis. More preplanning is now being done.

Note was taken of the stronger disposition by American firms to make capital expenditures. Walters acknowledged that such outlays are looked upon with much more caution in Britain.

HOSIERY INDUSTRY

A strong recommendation was made by the team representing this industry for more realistic study of individual work loads by means of scientific job studies. The report emphasized that both British management and workers should readily accept the lessons behind productivity which have evolved from an environment quite different from the British pattern.[22]

Commenting on the team report, Mr. C. G. Groocock, a member of the team and General Secretary of the National Union of Hosiery Workers, observed that since the team visit to America the union of Hosiery Workers approved an investigation of work study methods, but held up decision on adoption of this approach. Groocock maintained that at present British production per man-hour is equal to or greater than the rate in America. The big difference in total output he found to be in the use of three shifts in the United States. In his opinion, family life and the economy generally would fare better with only two shifts per day. He regarded both British and American workers in the Hosiery industry as highly efficient.

On the subject of union-management relations, Groocock observed that union officials and management keep in daily communication. If any employee has a grievance, a company official will telephone the union district officer and they will discuss the issue in a room set aside for the purpose. A national joint industrial council is maintained in the Hosiery industry. Healthy industrial relations are maintained because of the close contact between management and unions within the districts. While wage negotiations are conducted at the national level, many other matters are settled inside the individual factories by consultation with the union district officers. In Groocock's opinion American hosiery companies would be delighted if they had an equally good relationship with the many union organizations negotiating for Hosiery workers in this country.

FOOTWEAR INDUSTRY

The report of the Footwear team particularly urged that greater use be made of time and motion studies, work simplification, and incentive plans. The team recommended also that more mechanization be applied to this industry.[23]

A member of the Footwear team was Mr. P. J. Crawford, General President of the National Union of Boot and Shoe Operatives. It was his estimation that the team visit to America stimulated the use of new methods, though the industry was already productivity conscious. The shoe trade in Britain is very similar to that in the United States in regard to machinery. In the vital factors of plant layout, however, Americans plan more carefully.

An important psychological change has taken place since the team visit. People are no longer satisfied with the old arrangements. Before the visit the unions expected the shoe companies to do all the thinking. Management also has had to change its attitude.

Differing from some previous British statements on this point, Crawford observed that with respect to wages the British worker, if given the opportunity, will earn as much as possible. At present his cost of living is high just for necessities. Opportunity to earn more will come through better planning and the companies will also gain. Today piecework is well established. In general Crawford regarded the wage structure in the British Shoe industry as much simpler than in America.

Unfortunately it is hard to adapt time and motion study to a well established piece rate plan and even companies are apprehensive toward an arbitrary system of new work study. Yet employers and unions have set up a time and motion study program committee which has held a number of sessions. In the first meeting the companies did not even know the terminology of work study. They have since developed a point of view on the subject. Local productivity committees are also being formed, but they depend for success on co-operative attitude by both companies and unions. Some unions claim that certain companies are dropping these committees. Crawford found no such difficulty in the Northampton district.

Since the British Shoe industry is in a concentrated area, it is necessary to have one uniform system for all in the industry. Crawford noted that in the absence of a national agreement the Union of Boot and Shoe Operatives meets all companies which want a time study program and negotiates union-company agreements. Conferences are held with the workers to gain their support. The result is that every factory operative is following the same method of work study. Hope is held out for a national agreement on the problem.

Three grades of skill are recognized in the Shoe industry. Industrial consultants determine categories of ability in the various grades and then they are given union acceptance if satisfactory. Crawford emphasized that there has been very little friction on this point. In 96 of 100 cases the union approves the time study for the trial period. The union acceptance is now regarded as a protective factor needed to get the worker's consent.

Crawford stressed that union-management arbitration prevails in the Shoe industry, with companies divided into arbitration districts. One board is located in Northampton. Statements of policy are set for each area and may differ between districts. While there is a basic wage rate, many operatives get a higher rate per day in the upper grades than a similar graded worker in a competitor's firm. Companies are now asking if the arbitration board method of rate fixing will break down with the coming of work study. Crawford believed that the board could still function, but he admitted that companies and workers are dubious. At present a number of firms are remote from arbitration board areas.

A research association in the industry is making notable progress toward standardizing the basic parts of footwear. Union representatives are members of this association as equal partners. Yet, of the 40 industrial research associations in Britain only 7 have union representatives. Crawford believes that not enough attention is given by many companies to the fabricated parts for manufactured products so that they could be linked more closely with motion study. In any case output has been rising in the last few years.

The Review on Productivity in the Footwear Industry published in 1953 by the British Productivity Council, noted that a large representation from the Union of Boot and Shoe Operatives took part in the Productivity Conference which discussed the team's report.[24] Mr. Crawford, President of the Union has been emphatic in his position that wider use of capital equipment in the industry is necessary before Britain's workers can be compared with those in other countries on the question of relative output. Crawford considers that unions during negotiations with employers must make it plain that modern methods of management are as integral a part of demands for collective bargaining as any other phase of this process.[25]

As an indication of the practical interest shown by the Boot and Shoe Union in productivity, a number of its officials and shop stewards have taken courses in work study and are endeavoring to extend its use. During the 1953 conference of this union hope was expressed that a national agreement might be reached on the terms by which work study would be applied to the whole shoe industry in the next few years.[26]

THE BRITISH TRADES UNION CONGRESS

As a supplement to the work of the regular productivity teams operating under the auspices of the Anglo-American Productivity Council, the British Trades Union Congress sent to America a specialist team composed of trade union officials. More than a score of detailed recommendations for British unions were contained in this team's report.

On the subject of industrial efficiency the team urged that British unions recognize more extensively the role played by motion studies and job evaluation in raising productivity. To that end the team suggested that the larger unions establish production engineering departments with trained engineers to protect and promote the interests of union members. A competent technical staff in production engineering was recommended for the T. U. C. headquarters and for regional districts. Thoroughly trained members of such staffs should in turn instruct workshop representatives in techniques of production. Unions were encouraged in the report to promote greater mechanization of industry as a means to a higher standard of living. To safeguard wages and employment, unions should be prepared to offer technical advice to companies which are facing a decline in profit margins.[27]

The secretary of this specialist team of Union Officials was Mr. Robert Harle of the Organization Department of the British Trades Union Congress. In commenting on the team report, Harle said the members felt it has brought to light some valuable lessons for Britain. He acknowledged that some critics have held that less attention might have been paid to psychological and social factors of American life, such as the role of the American housewife. The basic parts of the report, however, have been given approval. Harle realized that the recommendations should not be put into effect forthwith. More consideration must be given to adapting them to the British economy. In some of the other reports it has been felt that members of the teams representing operatives did not maintain a sufficiently critical attitude toward the management point of view.

Harle stressed that educational programs have long been sponsored by the Trades Union Congress. Before the team report courses were already being conducted in law, history, and administration for union members. The T. U. C. summer school is held at Oxford each year. It includes a broad course on industrial relations. Moreover, there are week-end schools for rank and file members. One half day of these sessions is given to subjects dealing with productivity.

The T. U. C. conducts a special one week course for full time and part time union officers on subjects dealing with management and production. A number of outside experts on industrial management give the benefit of their own experience. Effort is made to examine the trade union implications involved. Over 400 union officials take part in the one week course which has been in operation for over four years. On the whole a quite positive attitude is maintained. It is emphasized that union officials are in industry and they must know the problems in this area to protect the interests of union members. Attention is given to industrial relations and negotiation. To improve the effectiveness of bargaining, mock negotiations are encouraged. Sources of statistical information are made known to the union officials participating in the course.

As advanced training, four firms of industrial consultants provide courses in work study and general management for full time trade union officials. It is a fairly broad approach and in accordance with high standards. Trade union officials have been very favorably impressed and believe it helps them in negotiations.

A recent innovation according to Harle is a week-end conference which is held in any part of the country. Sections taken from the one week course are discussed at such conferences. The results have been very successful. Still, there is always the difficulty of overcoming the objection of union officials that they do not have time for such meetings.

Unions themselves are doing much in the way of educational programs. The Union of General and Municipal Workers has conducted one month courses in industrial relations and work study at 14 centers. By the end of the winter of 1953, over one thousand shop stewards and full time union officials had attended such courses. The Transport Workers' Union has also done much in this direction.

A number of unions, such as the Amalgamated Engineering Union, the second largest in Britain, conduct week-end schools similar in aim to the one week course sponsored by T. U. C. Other smaller unions co-operate with local educational authorities to provide training facilities for their members.

The outcome of this new trend in education is an increasing number of union officials who are qualified in the technical aspects of negotiation as they relate to scientific management. In all these matters while the T. U. C. provides facilities in the way of consulting services, the trade unions remain autonomous in deciding how such facilities shall be used. Harle noted that unions do not normally come to the T. U. C. about wage questions, though they may bring queries about certain phases of incentive plans.

The T. U. C. recognizes the need for greater output by British industry, but insists upon safeguards to insure that workers will get a fair share in the final product. Importance is placed on the need of full employment to convince workers of the advantage in greater output. A number of union officials are fully aware of the necessity to reduce costs and improve delivery dates. Moreover, there is no objection to time and motion studies as such. Yet disputes arise if men suffer wage decreases from job simplification. Members of the British team of Trades Union Officials found that in the United States the rank and file attitude toward time and motion studies was similar to that in Britain.

Harle believed that the miners were now facing up to the problem of uneconomical mining pits. A number of such mines have been closed down in Scotland. Here the question of transferring workers to new jobs becomes critical, especially in regard to men over 55. In general the miners realize that to continue on a competitive basis in this industry Britain must reduce the work force.

Harle noted that training within industry has been encouraged by the Government. In such courses job relations are considered through the case approach and stress is placed on improving the effectiveness of shop stewards by presenting them with time and motion problems to be solved.

It is revealing to note some comments made in 1953 by Mr. Tom O'Brien, M. P., then President of the British Trades Union Congress. On numerous occasions O'Brien has made strong public utterances on the necessity of raising production in Great Britain. In July of 1953, O'Brien appealed to those attending a conference of the National Union of Mineworkers to improve the position of their negotiators by increasing coal production. His statement anticipated an attempt by Communist elements in the union to demand an immediate pay raise regardless of the industry's status on finances or output. O'Brien favored a policy of caution and realism in regard to wage demands.

Defying the tradition of nonintervention for a guest delegate from outside the Mineworkers' union, he bluntly told the members at the conference that output must be increased to a level that will reasonably permit a higher return for the labor expended. While advising the miners not to cease the quest for better wages and working conditions, he appealed to them to work along with management on the technical side and redirect their energies so that increased production would justify such claims. It is worthy of note that following this statement of O'Brien the conference of the Mineworkers decided to withdraw without discussion the resolution calling for an all-round wage increase.

In April of the same year O'Brien urged a convention of Scottish trade unionists to accept changes by management which aim to increase efficiency and to abandon the old fear of working oneself out of a job. He warned that workers who look upon efficiency only as a matter of concern to management may find themselves sadly disillusioned later. O'Brien emphasized that greater efficiency and the nation's livelihood go together. He observed that it is not a matter of class issues, but blunt economic facts. The stakes involved are full employment, social security and an adequate living standard. O'Brien stressed that the latter has to be earned.

Elsewhere in his address to this Scottish union convention O'Brien made known that the T. U. C. wants more men from the shops to attend its work study courses and more union officials to take extended work-study training with approved firms of industrial consultants. Scientific developments to make work more productive, in O'Brien's opinion, means better earnings and output as well as less strain and fatigue.[28]

E. C. A. TRADE UNION TECHNICAL MISSION TO THE UNITED STATES

One of the members of this group which visited America in 1951 was Mr. H. E. Matthews, National Industrial Officer of the Union of General and Municipal Workers. In his interim report on this mission he made the observation that British unions will eventually be faced with the problems arising from the growth of "scientific management." Up to the present he observed that most British unions have avoided the full implications of this trend. To be realistic in dealing with management Matthews stated in his report that unions must become fully cognizant of modern production techniques so that they can analyze and constructively criticize data presented them by production engineers.

Commenting on developments in Britain two years after his visit to America, Matthews believed that the most important outcome from the visits to the United States was the broader education of both unions and management rather than the adoption of some new types of machine or methods. One aspect of this broader education concerned the vital need to increase the total output instead of merely arguing how it is to be shared. He was of the view that among union groups there is growing recognition that this need for greater output outranks in importance the day to day problems of industry.

As an example of new industrial methods Matthews noted that big stone quarries are now being equipped with mechanical stone crushing devices. Yet there are hundreds of small quarries where it is not economical to mechanize and a living is still being eked out from them by hand methods. Hence both efficient and inefficient units exist side by side. Because of the great number of small British companies, there is more caution than in America concerning new capital investment. Big investment outlays seem less prudent in Britain. While both sides of British industry favor use of the best machines and methods available, there is ever in mind the limitation of scope for the development of British industry.

Thus far chief emphasis has been placed on discussion, analysis, and assessing. Matthews believes, however, that much is being done to mould conditions for change and to educate the union and management groups involved. The goal is to find the optimum, the most efficient and economical scale of production, while being mindful of the peculiar circumstances surrounding each industry in Britain's island economy.

In regard to union administration, Matthews noted that dues payments of 6d a week permit no reserves for financing full time technicians to carry on union research, as can be done in America. Nevertheless, this small union income does allow at least the education of union leaders in new methods of production.

WHAT BRITISH WORKERS CAN DO

A dramatic indication that British workers can be as adaptable, ambitious, and progressive as their counterparts in America was demonstrated in the construction of the 100 million dollar oil refinery in England for a subsidiary of Standard Oil of New Jersey. The task was completed in 1951, almost six months ahead of schedule. Under the direction of an American, Robert Cole, and 70 American supervisors, 5,000 British workmen proceeded to show that it was unsafe to assume for long that what Americans could do in 100 man-hours would require 154 man-hours from Britons. By the time the job was done there was little need to assign a handicap to this British work force.

Experiencing fewer labor disputes than in about any other large scale construction job done in England, Cole pursued a policy of speedy settlement of grievances at the early stages. Operating as a completely unionized estab-

lishment, a single contract embraced all 12 unions working on the refinery.

The workers were particularly impressed by the American supervisors who to their amazement were on the job
before the workmen and stayed with them to the end of
the day. Note was taken that they never asked a man to
do a task which they would not do themselves. Workers
on this job learned to ask the supervisor to give a hand if
extra help was needed. By contrast, many British foremen
are more closely allied with the "white-collar" class and
are never addressed by their first names. An appointment
might well be required of a worker should he wish to see
a British supervisor.

In the course of construction, classes were conducted in
new techniques on welding, pipe bending, and insulation.
All save two percent of the 5,000 workers were above the
unskilled labor designation at the end of the job. One
craftsman who finished his apprenticeship 20 years earlier
declared that he had never learned anything new on a job
until he worked on this refinery.

Because of the highly mechanized facilities and the
careful planning of material flow, fatigue was reduced to
the minimum. Practically all the workers regarded the job
as one of the easiest they had ever encountered. Yet they
were always mindful that schedules had to be met as
planned.[29]

The impact in Britain of this feat of construction has
been so great that a summary of the study made of the
project for the British Institute of Management has been
printed on the front pages of many English newspapers.
Editorials have vigorously asserted that such an achievement can and should be repeated elsewhere in England.

THE BRITISH PRODUCTIVITY COUNCIL

Operating from its London offices at 21 Tothill Street, the British Productivity Council, the successor to the U. K. Section of the Anglo-American Council on Productivity, continues to apply the lessons learned by that earlier organization. Like its predecessor, the British Productivity Council represents jointly both management and unions. Covering all phases of industrial activity, the B. P. C. is nonpolitical and independent of Government control. In operation since early 1953, this organization seeks by every possible means to encourage the improvement of productivity throughout the economy of the United Kingdom. Finances for the work of the Council are contributed by its member organizations and by an equal grant from the British government.

The B. P. C. devotes much of its efforts to showing employers and trade union leaders the benefits they can obtain from working together for the common aim of increasing productivity and efficiency in industry. This objective was enthusiastically supported by the Trades Union Congress in 1953 and by its President, at that time, Mr. Tom O'Brien.

By September, 1954, almost 100 local productivity committees had been established with the help of the B. P. C. throughout Britain, Wales, and Scotland. While these committees do not have a rigid composition, the B. P. C. has suggested that they should have a fair representation of members from both unions and management; and when possible, at least one committee official should be a union member.[30]

Many of these local productivity committees have held large scale public meetings in such cities as Manchester, Liverpool, and Birmingham. Valuable results have been forthcoming when these initial contacts have been followed up by more direct encounters at industrial plants. With very few exceptions response to these committees from both employers and trade unionists has been excellent. In a number of the larger manufacturing areas either full time or part time secretaries are retained for these local productivity committees. Elsewhere, secretarial work has been of a voluntary nature.

Periodically the B. P. C. holds regional conferences to enable members of the local committees to exchange views on problems they are facing. This arrangement permits communication between representatives of different industries to discuss questions of general interest.[31]

The British Productivity Council reported that by the fall of 1954 the average circulation in the United Kingdom alone for the 67 productivity team reports was 7,000 and demand for them continues. Wide sales of the reports have also taken place on the Continent and in other parts of the world. Versions of the team reports have been translated into numerous languages. Based on reviews made by B. P. C. for several industries which sent productivity teams to America, it appears that a large number of the firms in such industries are acting in accordance with the recommendations made in the teams' reports.

BRITISH PRODUCTIVITY SINCE THE TEAM VISITS

It was estimated in 1952 that British productivity amounted to one-half the rate in America.[32] In large part this great disparity can be traced to the enormous superiority in mechanical investment and to the extensive use of planning in the United States. Britain has much ground to cover before she will compare favorably with the United States on these points.

Nevertheless, there are indications that output per worker is increasing. By dividing an index of industrial employment into an index of industrial production, it has been estimated that productivity in manufacturing increased about 4 to 5 percent a year from the first half of 1948 to the first half of 1951. In the second half of 1951, however, it was no greater than the year before and in 1952 there was a temporary decline in productivity to 3 or 4 percent below that of 1951. By 1953, this loss had been recovered and output was again at the high level of 1951. Apparently the main reason for the decline in 1952 was a drop in demand, first in the domestic market and later overseas.[33]

Chancellor of the Exchequer R. A. Butler in November, 1954, stated to the National Union of Manufacturers that Britain was making good progress towards the goal of economic expansion without inflation. He noted that this goal involves three concepts: higher productivity, greater exports, and more productive investments. On the point of productivity, Butler declared that by mid-1954 the rate of industrial production had risen 8 percent over a period of 12 months while the number of workers added was only 3 percent. In the fall of 1954 more people than ever were at work and unemployment was at a "very low" figure.[34]

It would be quite impossible to isolate from many other factors the influence of the team reports on British productivity since the war. In many instances developments toward greater productivity had been under way before the teams visited America. Nevertheless, representatives from both management and unions are ready to acknowledge the notable progress towards a stronger British economy which has resulted from the work of the productivity teams.

CHAPTER SEVEN

Appraisal and Prospects

To emphasize the main factors which appear to be responsible for the high rate of productivity in the United States, the British Productivity Council in 1953 published a series of tables listing the frequency with which significant characteristics of the American industrial economy were mentioned in 58 Productivity team reports. Findings from that analysis will be referred to at various stages of this chapter.

MANAGEMENT POLICIES ON INDUSTRIAL RELATIONS

According to the B. P. C. analysis, 22 of the British Productivity team reports listed cordial relations between management and workers as a main factor accountable for high productivity in America. It should be observed that this characteristic, as true of others, was often mentioned by other teams as well, but in 22 of the reports it was regarded as a principal factor behind high output.[1]

Frequent surprise, however, was expressed at the existence of a written contract between individual companies and unions. While in Britain national agreements prevail between employer associations and national unions, most understandings involving union locals and individual companies are on an informal basis with only a verbal record.

Nevertheless, the degree of autonomy exercised by American union locals and management, as a result of written contracts, appears to be much greater than is commonly the case between unions and companies in Britain. This greater stress on local bargaining in America as compared to national bargaining was listed by 15 of the team reports as a significant factor promoting high output in America.[2] Considerable advantage in planning production was seen in the existence of a fixed wage clause in contracts, as well as a no strike clause. In Britain wage issues may be brought up at any time.

Most of the teams, however, expressed strong preference for the British practice of industry wide bargaining on the grounds that it avoided excessive duplication of effort and loss of time which seemed to be inevitable under local bargaining. It should be noted that while regional and industry wide bargaining in this country relate to the minority of union membership, the trend shows an increase as relationships with unions become more mature in various industries.

Despite the wide use of joint consultation procedures in British factories by which management and worker representatives meet to discuss certain problem areas in the plant, it seems evident that there is a far wider knowledge possessed by workers on company matters in American plants than is true in Britain. Twenty of the British productivity teams remarked on the benefits derived from the willingness of American management to disclose company information to employees.[3] Actually the sessions on joint consultation between British workers and management often do not touch on methods of production. Their usual areas of discussion relate to absenteeism, labor turnover, health conditions, safety, and welfare.

Yet the greater frankness of American management in discussing company policy with workers should not be construed as a noticeable trend toward what might be called union-management co-operation on methods of production. Save in certain hard pressed cases American unions are seldom asked for advice on such matters. Even during World War II, only 500 of the 5,000 labor-management committees organized under the sponsorship of the War Production Board really gave significant attention to methods of production. The bulk of these committees devoted most of their efforts to activities similar to the British joint consultation groups. Moreover, by 1948 the total number of the committees had shrunk from 5,000 to 300.[4]

It is apparent that as long as American management continues to maintain a strong lead in improving methods of production, union organizations will be content to evaluate such changes in terms of their effect on union members and then take whatever action seems appropriate. That the initiative in this area is still securely in the hands of company representatives was the conclusion of 30 British productivity teams which held that the progressive attitude of American management is a prime factor responsible for the high level of productivity in this country.[5]

In contrast with the rather staid tempo which induces many firms in Britain to follow traditional patterns of pro-

duction, 33 of the British team concluded that a strong
spirit of competition is a notable factor accounting for the
high industrial output in America.[6] Of course this competition does not resemble the classical concept of many
sellers marketing an identical product. Instead it is better
described as a fierce rivalry amongst industrial concentrates. Each firm is aware that its economic position may
decline unless constant efforts are made to improve methods of production, and the attractiveness of the product.
Accordingly management in America has put great stress
on what the British call work study, which was cited by
33 of the team reports and work simplification, noted by
24 of the team reports.[7] In general the term work study
embraces the minutely accurate efforts to measure industrial processes and operation in order to avoid waste of
effort and improve work flow. British management and
unions have just begun to recognize how much productivity depends on proficiency in such areas.

In the B. P. C. analysis of the productivity reports it was
found that 43 of the teams regarded the extensive use of
mechanical aids as a significant element bearing on the
high industrial output in the United States.[8] Prolonged depression and heavy physical and financial loss from two
World Wars have reinforced the natural tendency of British management to extend the life span of obsolescent
capital equipment. Yet a salient development from the
team visits to America have been efforts by British union
officials to impress on management the importance of more
mechanical aids in production.

On the point of new capital equipment, the disparity
between Britain and the United States will soon be marked
off even more sharply as automation makes further inroads
into American factories. This new technological trend by

which machines are installed to operate other machines requires enormous capital investment. Proportionately, Britain is still far behind the United States in the use of ordinary power tools.

Role of Unions in Industrial Relations

Though many leaders in British unions have developed a high degree of maturity in dealing with public issues in their country, they have acknowledged that union officials in America often are better versed in the technical problems facing individual companies. In 22 of the team reports belief was expressed that a strong sense of cost consciousness at all levels of operation was a primary factor in American industry.[9] Straight demands for wage increases, accompanied by opposition to changes in methods of production, is an indication that sensitivity to cost factors is not too well developed amongst British workers. The need for higher productivity, in the estimation of 43 of the British teams, is apparent to American workers without the preliminary of an indoctrination program.[10]

Moreover, American unions generally are aware of the important role played by management in raising the levels of output. It is revealing to note that while British union officials willingly pay tribute to the talents of American management, their remarks are by no means so complimentary when speaking of the initiative of British industrial officials on this point.

Belief in change was a characteristic of American life which 28 British teams considered a strong factor underlying high productivity.[11] Laborsaving devices are accepted as inevitable, even though they may mean serious temporary dislocations.[12] A far greater resistance to new methods is displayed by British unions. Many obsolete union working rules are still rigidly adhered to out of fear that severe unemployment might follow if they were relaxed. Unlike in America where unions generally have modified their membership standards to cope with mass production techniques, many craft unions in Britain refuse to modify their structures though the bargaining power of the craftsman is steadily declining because of this intransigence. Even within the same craft union it is sometimes required that British workers get another membership card before being admitted to a different subdivision of the same union.

It is of interest that many of the teams which commented on the seniority rule, spoke of it unfavorably and few team reports listed seniority as a device to increase productivity. In actuality, because of the steady trend towards increased output in America, one might question if the dire effects from seniority feared by the British have much foundation.

THE NEW APPROACH BY BRITISH UNIONS

Traditional patterns of thinking in many British unions are undergoing heavy attack because of the lessons learned from the team visits to America. Efforts are now being made to get general acceptance by unions of scientific methods of production in the belief that the results will noticeably raise output and the share of income going to workers. Knowledge of the techniques of scientific management is now considered a prerequisite for union officials to enable them to strengthen their bargaining position with management. Ignorance of this development in modern industry is regarded as a threat to the best interests of union members.

Based on their observations in America, the team appointed by the Productivity Council to study Materials Handling recommended that unions in Britain should welcome any effort to install better methods of handling materials by mechanical means or otherwise.[13] A member of the executive committee of the Amalgamated Union of Foundry Workers, Mr. R. Casasola, stated that union members in the United Kingdom should become aware of the need for new industrial developments. He declared that British unions must show a readiness to accept changes in methods which even may bring a reduction of the work force in particular cases, or which may break down certain skilled jobs into easier tasks requiring less training.[14] As its first recommendation the report of the specialist team on Welding urged that management extend its economic planning and mechanization. In regard to the unions, this report stressed that labor saving devices should be accepted with a "realistic" approach to any redundancy of workers which might result.[15]

The special report on Productivity by British Trade Union Officials asserted that in the future unions in England must assume a "new industrial role." Where managements make use of scientific methods in a progressive manner to increase production, the unions involved should give their co-operation. If the scientific technique is pushed beyond reasonable bounds, while still not opposing the new methods, the unions should endeavor to have the abuses and inaccuracies of the scientific approach eliminated so that they will not cause economic loss to the operatives. Concerning the laggard companies, the unions must exert the necessary pressure to get them in line.[16]

Until recent years the willingness of American union leaders to negotiate with management in the realm of so-called scientific methods was taken in Britain as indication of subservience. Today the old notion that American unions are merely "the tools of management" is in its death throes. Not a few British unions are now subscribers to services on scientific methods provided by the British Institute of Management. Mr. P. J. Crawford, President of the National Union of Boot and Shoe Operatives, and a member of the T. U. C. General Council, has stated publicly that unions must adjust themselves to the trends of modern industry and be in position to negotiate with management on the new methods of operation.[17]

The immediate concern facing many British unions is the need to train staffs for industrial research departments; and union officials who will be qualified to discuss problems with management which bear on modern methods of production. For adequate proficiency, it is believed that intensive courses of three or four months' duration will be necessary. Results have not been too satisfactory from making use of mere week-end programs or even courses lasting a fortnight.

A serious obstacle which must be overcome, if staffs are to be properly trained, is the need to build up union finances. At present union revenues are woefully inadequate to permit any great development of research departments and of three months' training programs. Dues will have to be increased considerably before British unions can advance in this work. Thus far not much has been done in this direction. Funds have been sufficient to finance only three months' training courses for a relatively few union officials. To obtain general acceptability of new industrial methods by the rank and file membership in British unions, a much greater number of union leaders will have to become versed in the new techniques by intensive study programs.

COMPARATIVE WAGE STANDARDS

It was the conclusion of 28 of the team reports that a desire for a better standard of living directly relates to the high level of output in the United States.[18] Nevertheless, the question was raised whether it is realistic to assume that a single American standard of living prevails throughout the country. Too many variations in levels of living, both regionally and locally, were observed by the team members. Note was also taken of the tendency for wage earners in America to mortgage their future income for two or three years at a time in order to enjoy some of the possessions commonly identified with the American standard of living.[19]

Nevertheless 24 of the British teams regarded the high level of real wages in America as a prime factor accounting for the exceptional rate of productivity here.[20] Bearing out this same observation, 25 of the team reports spoke of the abundance of consumer goods in this country available at reasonable prices.[21] There is strong evidence to conclude that it takes 2 to 4 times more work hours in Britain than in America to obtain the purchasing power necessary to acquire many common items of food, clothing and other personal needs. Moreover, tax levies in this country have a milder impact on wage earner income and do not increase as sharply when wage rates are raised.

Eleven of the team reports spoke of the simpler wage structure prevailing in America as compared with Britain.[22] The widespread use of straight hourly pay methods prevents much confusion in trying to estimate one's weekly earnings. In England the highly complex wage patterns growing out of the use of incentive plans makes it difficult to calculate future earnings. In 1951 workers in a British pressed metal plant had to allow for 13 separate wage items before they could determine the amount to expect in their pay envelopes.[23] It is true that in American industry graded differentials may exist for the same job according to one's degree of proficiency. This type of wage structure, however, is readily understood and tends to stimulate greater effort.

Despite serious handicaps the distribution of income in Britain has greatly improved during the postwar period. In 1954 average earnings had increased 61 percent above the level of 1947.[24] A greater percentage of consumer goods is presently being purchased by the British public. Though profit returns are high, it is believed that most of them are now being expended for modern factory construction and equipment.

Nevertheless, many wage earners in Britain are restive because of the long wage freeze in the face of improved economic conditions. Average wages are well below $30 per week.[25] Work stoppages on a large scale loom ahead unless wage increases are forthcoming. As one example, the National Union of Railwaymen has threatened to strike unless increases from $1.12 to $1.32 per week are granted to workers who presently earn from $17.78 to $24.78 per week.[26]

VARIED VIEWS ON WAYS TO SHARE INCOME

As an important factor encouraging higher productivity, 13 of the team reports cited the lack of hostility by organized labor in America toward the earning of profits by employers.[27] In contrast British unions have been extremely suspicious of profit-taking by companies. It must

not be overlooked though, that British firms in the past
have frequently shown little disposition to improve wage
rates along with better dividend disbursements. Moreover,
when savings were made by improved methods of production British wage earners have not realized much advantage through higher wages. Accordingly, British unions
have found little basis for identifying a company making
good profits with one which will grant appreciable advantages at the bargaining table.

Though profitable companies were viewed favorably by
American unions the British teams found that little enthusiasm was shown toward profit sharing plans for employees. It is significant that despite a hundred-year history behind this method of distributing income to workers,
a survey of 16,000 manufacturing companies in 1945–46
revealed that less than 2 percent paid profit sharing bonuses to their workers. The heavy toll taken of such
schemes in time of depression and the uncertainty of income from them because of circumstances beyond the
control of workers have confined their existence to a relatively small group of companies. In many cases, special
characteristics of these concerns make them particularly
suitable for profit sharing plans.[28]

As an alternative even to piece rate methods and incentive schemes the British teams found that predominant
preference by American unions pointed in the direction of
straight hourly wage rates. Various types of incentive plans,
however, are far more prevalent in America than are
profit sharing schemes. Nevertheless, incentive payments
are by no means as widely used in the United States as in
Britain.

Only 13 of the 58 team reports examined by the British
Productivity Council regarded incentive plans as of sig-

nificant importance in accounting for the high rate of American productivity.[29] A common attitude toward these plans, especially on the part of union representatives, was based on the objection that they exacted too high a charge in physical strain and worker rivalry. The minor status of incentive plans in America contrasts sharply with their widespread application in Great Britain. In that country the opinion remains strong that higher output depends primarily on greater physical output of individual workers. Yet in America where production is far higher per employee, great stress is placed on careful work planning and flow of materials so that in effect physical effort of each worker is actually lessened as the rate of output increases. Britain puts hope in the possibility that incentive plans, by inducing greater physical exertion, will counterbalance in some degree the enormous outlay of capital investment which is constantly being made in American industry.

VOLUME OF PRODUCTION

The rise of industrial output in Britain between the years 1948 and 1953 compares very well with the American picture. Britain's index of industrial production in May, 1954 was 32 percent above the level of 1948.[30] In 1953 the American index of industrial production was 34 percent above the 1947–49 level.[31] The Britain Federation of Iron and Steel trades reported a rise in steel production of 45 percent from the end of World War II to 1954. In the view of the Federation this expansion was fully proportionate to the progress made in the American steel industry.[32]

Note should be taken that Drew Middleton, writing for

the *New York Times* from London, observed that two forces which are given credit for the present efficiency of British industrial production are the severity of German and Japanese competition and the reports of the Anglo-American productivity teams.[33] Of course the total volume of industrial output in America is on a much greater scale than is true of England. Moreover, Britain is in no position to match the enormous sum of $150 billion which American industry has poured into plant replacements since World War II.[34]

It would be unwise, however, to assume that a wholesale transplanting of American plant facilities and methods to England would be a proper course of action; a proposal favored by some Americans. Prosperity for Britain is dependent on adjustment to a quite different set of circumstances. A relatively stationary population exists in Britain compared to our rapid upward trend. Many vast areas in America are still on the threshold of development. Britain by comparison is a small island already at a high stage of maturity. All these factors tend to militate against economic expansion in Britain on a scale comparable with America.

Nevertheless, numerous adaptations from American industrial techniques can well be applied to the British economy and the propitious time to make the applications is the present. With unassigned workers numbering only 250,000, or 1 percent of the work force, conditions are most favorable for adopting new machinery and work methods which will economize on manpower and decrease costs.[35]

The British percentage of unemployment contrasts sharply with the American figure of over 4 per cent in 1954, or more than three million workers.[36] It is of interest that during the summer of 1953 great anxiety was felt in Britain that even a moderate drop in employment in America might cause a disproportionately great decline in British employment because of the probable impact on world trade. Actually the British economy continued to improve steadily despite the moderate American recession in 1954. Greater British trade on the European continent easily made up for the decrease in exports to the United States.

FOOTNOTES

Chapter One

1. Anglo-American Council on Productivity, *Report of the First Session,* London, November, 1948, p. 1.
2. *The Final Report of the Anglo-American Council on Productivity,* London, 1952, p. 39.
3. Anglo-American Council on Productivity, *Report of the First Session, op. cit.,* p. 4.
4. *The Final Report of the Anglo-American Council on Productivity, op. cit.,* p. 2.
5. *Ibid.,* p. 8.
6. *Ibid.,* p. 10.
7. *Ibid.,* p. 20.
8. *Ibid.,* p. 14.
9. *Ibid.,* pp. 20, 23.
10. *Ibid.,* p. 10.
11. *Ibid.*
12. *Ibid.,* p. 28.
13. *Ibid.,* p. 29.
14. *Ibid.,* p. 11.
15. *Ibid.*
16. *Ibid.,* p. 3.

Chapter Two

1. Productivity Team Report, *Ammunition,* London, 1953, p. 38.
2. Productivity Team Report, *Packet Foods,* London, 1951, p. 31.

3. Productivity Team Report, *Cakes and Biscuits*, London, 1952, p. 42.
4. Productivity Team Report, *Machine Tools*, London, 1953, p. 28.
5. Productivity Team Report, *Internal Combustion Engines*, London, 1950, p. 10.
6. *Ibid.*
7. Productivity Team Report, *Pharmaceuticals*, London, 1951, p. 64.
8. Productivity Team Report, *Brassfoundry*, London, 1951, p. 8.
9. Productivity Team Report, *Machine Tools*, *op. cit.*, p. 28.
10. Productivity Team Report, *Valves*, London, 1951, p. 7.
11. Productivity Team Report, *Brassfoundry*, *op. cit.*, p. 9.
12. Productivity Team Report, *Cotton Spinning*, London, 1950, p. 17.
13. Productivity Team Report, *Furniture*, London, April 1952, p. 62.
14. Productivity Team Report, *Steel Founding*, London, 1949, p. 11.
15. Productivity Team Report, *Pressed Metals*, London, 1950, p. 46.
16. Productivity Team Report, *Non-Ferrous Metals*, London, 1951, p. 14.
17. Productivity Team Report, *Food Canning*, London, 1952, p. 65.
18. Productivity Team Report, *Pharmaceuticals*, *op. cit.*, pp. 64, 65.
19. *Trade Unions and Productivity*, London, 1949, p. 57.
20. Productivity Team Report, *Cotton Yarn Doubling*, London, 1950, pp. 11, 12.
21. Productivity Team Report, *Food Canning*, *op. cit.*, p. 63.
22. Productivity Team Report, *Cakes and Biscuits*, *op. cit.*, p. 46.
23. Productivity Team Report, *Footwear*, London, October 1951, pp. 49, 50.
24. Productivity Team Report, *Meat Packaging and Processing*, London, 1951, p. 48.
25. *Trade Unions and Productivity*, *op. cit.*, p. 48.
26. *Ibid.*, p. 57.
27. Productivity Team Report, *Electricity Supply*, London, 1950, p. 69.
28. *Ibid.*, pp. 69, 70.
29. Productivity Team Report, *Cotton Spinning*, *op. cit.*, p. 20.
30. Productivity Team Report, *Coal*, London, 1951, p. 19.
31. Productivity Team Report, *Pressed Metals*, *op. cit.*, 47.
32. Productivity Team Report, *Cotton Yarn Doubling*, *op. cit.*, p. 12.
33. Productivity Team Report, *Diesel Locomotives*, London, 1950, p. 36.
34. Productivity Team Report, *Cotton Yarn Doubling*, *op. cit.*, p. 12.
35. Productivity Team Report, *Internal Combustion Engines*, *op. cit.*, p. 10.
36. Productivity Team Report, *Iron and Steel*, London, 1952, p. 79.
37. Productivity Team Report, *Electricity Supply*, *op. cit.*, p. 66.
38. Productivity Team Report, *Building*, London, 1950, pp. 56, 57.
39. Productivity Team Report, *Welding*, London, 1951, pp. 40, 41.
40. Productivity Team Report, *Internal Combustion Engines*, *op. cit.*, pp. 13, 14.
41. Productivity Team Report, *Lithographic Printing*, London, October 1951, p. 51.
42. Productivity Team Report, *Cotton Weaving*, *op. cit.*, pp. 8, 9.
43. Productivity Team Report, *Grey Ironfounding*, London, 1950, p. 36.

44. Productivity Team Report, *Ammunition, op. cit.*, p. 48.
45. Productivity Team Report, *Building, op. cit.*, p. 56.
46. Productivity Team Report, *Brassfoundry, op. cit.*, p. 9.
47. Productivity Team Report, *Footwear, op. cit.*, p. 53.
48. Productivity Team Report, *Freight Handling,* London, 1951, p. 44.
49. Productivity Team Report, *Coal, op. cit.*, p. 18.
50. Productivity Team Report, *Iron and Steel, op. cit.*, p. 74.
51. Productivity Team Report, *Internal Combustion Engines, op. cit.*, p. 11.
52. Productivity Team Report, *Building, op. cit.*, p. 57.
53. Productivity Team Report, *Cotton Yarn Doubling, op. cit.*, p. 45.

Chapter Three

1. Productivity Team Report, *Cotton Spinning, op. cit.*, p. 17.
2. Productivity Team Report, *Welding, op. cit.*, pp. 44, 45.
3. Productivity Team Report, *Materials Handling in Industry,* London, 1949, p. 39.
4. Productivity Team Report, *Grey Ironfounding, op. cit.*, p. 32.
5. Productivity Team Report, *Cotton Spinning, op. cit.*, p. 15.
6. *Ibid.*
7. *Trade Unions and Productivity, op. cit.*, p. 51.
8. *Ibid.*, p. 56.
9. Productivity Team Report, *Valves, op. cit.*, p. 9.
10. Productivity Team Report, *Welding, op. cit.*, p. 47.
11. Productivity Team Report, *Cotton Yarn Doubling, op. cit.*, p. 47.
12. Productivity Team Report, *Rayon Weaving,* London, 1949, p. 14.
13. Productivity Team Report, *Welding, op. cit.*, p. 53.
14. *Trade Unions and Productivity, op. cit.*, p. 52.
15. *Ibid.*
16. Productivity Team Report, *Brushes,* London, 1951, p. 11.
17. Productivity Team Report, *Cotton Yarn Doubling, op. cit.*, p. 44.
18. Productivity Team Report, *Coal, op. cit.*, p. 16.
19. *Trade Unions and Productivity, op. cit.*, pp. 49, 50.
20. Productivity Team Report, *Coal, op. cit.*, p. 30.
21. *Ibid.*
22. Productivity Team Report, *Freight Handling, op. cit.*, p. 45.
23. *Ibid.*, p. 43.
24. Productivity Team Report, *Brushes, op. cit.*, p. 8.
25. Productivity Team Report, *Valves, op. cit.*, p. 9.
26. Productivity Team Report, *Ammunition, op. cit.*, p. 41.
27. Productivity Team Report, *Steel Construction,* London, 1952, p. 60.
28. Productivity Team Report, *Pharmaceuticals, op. cit.*, p. 64.
29. Productivity Team Report, *Internal Combustion Engines, op. cit.*, p. 12.
30. Productivity Team Report, *Grey Ironfounding, op. cit.*, p. 33.
31. Productivity Team Report, *Meat Packaging and Processing, op. cit.*, p. 51.

202 BRITAIN VIEWS OUR INDUSTRIAL RELATIONS

32. Productivity Team Report, *Food Canning, op. cit.,* p. 66.
33. Productivity Team Report, *Ammunition, op. cit.,* p. 42.
34. Productivity Team Report, *Furniture, op. cit.,* p. 63.
35. Productivity Team Report, *Cakes and Biscuits, op. cit.,* p. 47.
36. Productivity Team Report, *Brushes, op. cit.,* p. 8.
37. Productivity Team Report, *Food Canning, op. cit.,* p. 65.
38. Productivity Team Report, *Ammunition, op. cit.,* p. 44.
39. Productivity Team Report, *Welding, op. cit.,* p. 43.
40. *Ibid.,* p. 52.
41. Productivity Team Report, *Internal Combustion Engines, op. cit.,* p. 12.
42. Productivity Team Report, *Machine Tools, op. cit.,* p. 28.
43. Productivity Team Report, *Steel Founding, op. cit.,* p. 11.
44. Productivity Team Report, *Welding, op. cit.,* p. 40.
45. Productivity Team Report, *Internal Combustion Engines, op. cit.,* p. 13.
46. Productivity Team Report, *Footwear, op. cit.,* pp. 51, 52.
47. Productivity Team Report, *Pressed Metals, op. cit.,* p. 45.
48. Productivity Team Report, *Electricity Supply, op. cit.,* p. 67.
49. *Trade Unions and Productivity, op. cit.,* p. 52.
50. Productivity Team Report, *Electric Motor Control Gear,* London, 1950, p. 32.
51. Productivity Team Report, *Rigid Boxes and Cartons,* London, 1951, p. 5.
52. Productivity Team Report, *Furniture, op. cit.,* p. 63.
53. Productivity Team Report, *Milk Utilisation,* London, 1953, p. 91.
54. Productivity Team Report, *Valves, op. cit.,* p. 11.
55. Productivity Team Report, *Welding, op. cit.,* pp. 40, 41.
56. Productivity Team Report, *Cotton Yarn Doubling, op. cit.,* p. 12.
57. *Trade Unions and Productivity, op. cit.,* p. 24.
58. Productivity Team Report, *Cotton Spinning, op. cit.,* p. 17.
59. *Trade Unions and Productivity, op. cit.,* pp. 34, 35.
60. *Ibid.,* pp. 26, 27.
61. *Ibid.,* pp. 30, 31.
62. *Ibid.,* p. 32.
63. *Ibid.,* p. 43.
64. *Ibid.*
65. *Ibid.,* p. 49.
66. Productivity Team Report, *Coal, op. cit.,* p. 19.
67. *Trade Unions and Productivity, op. cit.,* p. 49.
68. Productivity Team Report, *Welding, op. cit.,* pp. 42, 43.
69. Productivity Team Report, *Furniture, op. cit.,* p. 63.
70. Productivity Team Report, *Welding, op. cit.,* pp. 42, 43.
71. Productivity Team Report, *Footwear, op. cit.,* pp. 50, 51.
72. Productivity Team Report, *Welding, op. cit.,* p. 43.
73. Productivity Team Report, *Furniture, op. cit.,* p. 62.
74. Productivity Team Report, *Coal, op. cit.,* p. 18.
75. Productivity Team Report, *Non-Ferrous Metals, op. cit.,* p. 15.
76. Productivity Team Report, *Welding, op. cit.,* p. 45.

77. Productivity Team Report, *Internal Combustion Engines, op. cit.,* p. 13.
78. Productivity Team Report, *Brassfoundry, op. cit.,* p. 9.
79. *Ibid.,* p. 8.
80. Productivity Team Report, *Rigid Boxes and Cartons, op. cit.,* p. 2.
81. Productivity Team Report, *Packet Foods, op. cit.,* p. 33.
82. Productivity Team Report, *Footwear, op. cit.,* p. 53.
83. Productivity Team Report, *Welding, op. cit.,* p. 43.
84. Productivity Team Report, *Iron and Steel, op. cit.,* p. 79.
85. Productivity Team Report, *Ammunition, op. cit.,* p. 42.
86. *Trade Unions and Productivity, op. cit.,* p. 48.
87. *Ibid.,* p. 50.
88. *Ibid.,* pp. 47, 48.
89. Productivity Team Report, *Building, op. cit.,* p. 55.
90. *Trade Unions and Productivity, op. cit.,* p. 47.
91. Productivity Team Report, *Welding, op. cit.,* p. 53.
92. *Trade Unions and Productivity, op. cit.,* p. 11.
93. *Ibid.,* p. 51.
94. Productivity Team Report, *Fruit and Vegetable Utilisation,* London, 1952, p. 46.

Chapter Four

1. Productivity Team Report, *Brassfoundry, op. cit.,* p. 6.
2. *Trade Unions and Productivity, op. cit.,* p. 58.
3. *Ibid.*
4. *Ibid.,* p. 55.
5. *Ibid.,* p. 28.
6. Productivity Team Report, *Welding, op. cit.,* p. 47.
7. Productivity Team Report, *Brushes, op. cit.,* p. 10.
8. Productivity Team Report, *Letterpress Printing,* London, 1951, p. 10.
9. Productivity Team Report, *Pressed Metal, op. cit.,* p. 45.
10. Productivity Team Report, *Coal, op. cit.,* p. 22.
11. *Ibid.,* p. 21.
12. Productivity Team Report, *Internal Combustion Engines, op. cit.,* p. 12.
13. *Trade Unions and Productivity, op. cit.,* p. 45.
14. *Ibid.,* p. 12.
15. *Ibid.,* p. 54.
16. Productivity Team Report, *Building, op. cit.,* p. 52.
17. *Trade Unions and Productivity, op. cit.,* p. 54.
18. Productivity Team Report, *Electricity Supply, op. cit.,* p. 65.
19. Productivity Team Report, *Food Canning, op. cit.,* pp. 66, 67.
20. Productivity Team Report, *Cotton Spinning, op. cit.,* p. 18.
21. *Ibid.,* p. 88.
22. Productivity Team Report, *Building, op. cit.,* p. 53.
23. Productivity Team Report, *Letterpress Printing, op. cit.,* p. 11.
24. Productivity Team Report, *Furniture, op. cit.,* p. 65.

25. Productivity Team Report, *Grey Ironfounding, op. cit.,* pp. 92, 93.
26. *Ibid.,* p. 93.
27. Productivity Team Report, *Letterpress Printing, op. cit.,* p. 10.
28. Productivity Team Report, *Diesel Locomotives, op. cit.,* p. 36.
29. Productivity Team Report, *Brassfoundry, op. cit.,* p. 6.
30. *Trade Unions and Productivity, op. cit.,* pp. 13, 14.
31. Productivity Team Report, *Building, op. cit.,* pp. 53, 54.
32. Productivity Team Report, *Welding, op. cit.,* p. 47.
33. Productivity Team Report, *Brassfoundry, op. cit.,* p. 6.
34. Productivity Team Report, *Internal Combustion Engines, op. cit.,* p. 7.
35. *Ibid.*
36. Productivity Team Report, *Steel Founding, op. cit.,* p. 13.
37. Productivity Team Report, *Cotton Yarn Doubling, op. cit.,* p. 13.
38. Productivity Team Report, *Coal, op. cit.,* p. 24.
39. *Trade Unions and Productivity, op. cit.,* p. 13.
40. Productivity Team Report, *Welding, op. cit.,* p. 41.
41. Productivity Team Report, *Building, op. cit.,* p. 55.
42. Productivity Team Report, *Rigid Boxes and Cartons, op. cit.,* p. 2.
43. Productivity Team Report, *Rayon Weaving, op. cit.,* p. 15.
44. Productivity Team Report, *Brassfoundry, op. cit.,* p. 3.
45. Productivity Team Report, *Men's Clothing, op. cit.,* p. 30.
46. Productivity Team Report, *Iron and Steel, op. cit.,* p. 82.

Chapter Five

1. Productivity Team Report, *Building, op. cit.,* p. 55.
2. *Trade Unions and Productivity, op. cit.,* pp. 52, 53.
3. Productivity Team Report, *Fruit and Vegetable Utilisation, op. cit.,* p. 46.
4. Productivity Team Report, *Footwear, op. cit.,* p. 52.
5. Productivity Team Report, *Meat Packaging and Processing, op. cit.,* p. 71.
6. Productivity Team Report, *Letterpress Printing, op. cit.,* p. 11.
7. *Ibid.*
8. *Trade Unions and Productivity, op. cit.,* p. 10.
9. Productivity Team Report, *Cakes and Biscuits, op. cit.,* p. 44.
10. Productivity Team Report, *Packet Foods, op. cit.,* p. 33.
11. Productivity Team Report, *Rigid Boxes and Cartons, op. cit.,* p. 4.
12. Productivity Team Report, *Freight Handling, op. cit.,* p. 46.
13. Productivity Team Report, *Internal Combustion Engines, op. cit.,* p. 49.
14. Productivity Team Report, *Meat Packaging and Processing, op. cit.,* p. 51.
15. Productivity Team Report, *Furniture, op. cit.,* p. 64.
16. Productivity Team Report, *Electric Motor Control Gear, op. cit.,* p. 31.
17. Productivity Team Report, *Brushes, op. cit.,* p. 9.

18. Productivity Team Report, *Electricity Supply, op. cit.,* p. 66.
19. *Trade Unions and Productivity, op. cit.,* p. 10.
20. Productivity Team Report, *Valves, op. cit.,* p. 12.
21. Productivity Team Report, *Welding, op. cit.,* p. 50.
22. Productivity Team Report, *Men's Clothing, op. cit.,* p. 6.
23. *Ibid.,* p. 30.
24. Productivity Team Report, *Internal Combustion Engines, op. cit.,* p. 11.
25. Productivity Team Report, *Cotton Yarn Doubling, op. cit.,* p. 10.
26. Productivity Team Report, *Grey Ironfounding, op. cit.,* p. 32.
27. Productivity Team Report, *Footwear, op. cit.,* p. 48.
28. *Ibid.,* pp. 49, 50.
29. *Ibid.,* p. 48.
30. Productivity Team Report, *Non-Ferrous Metals, op. cit.,* p. 15.
31. *Trade Unions and Productivity, op. cit.,* p. 54.
32. Productivity Team Report, *Meat Packaging and Processing, op. cit.,* p. 51.
33. *Ibid.,* p. 70.
34. Productivity Team Report, *Food Canning, op. cit.,* p. 68.
35. Productivity Team Report, *Cotton Yarn Doubling, op. cit.,* p. 15.
36. Productivity Team Report, *Pressed Metals, op. cit.,* p. 45.
37. *Trade Unions and Productivity, op. cit.,* p. 19.
38. *Ibid.*
39. Productivity Team Report, *Meat Packaging and Processing, op. cit.,* p. 49.
40. *Trade Unions and Productivity, op. cit.,* p. 19.
41. Productivity Team Report, *Coal, op. cit.,* pp. 25, 26.
42. *Ibid.,* p. 26.
43. *Ibid.,* p. 27.
44. *Trade Unions and Productivity, op. cit.,* p. 14.
45. Productivity Team Report, *Electricity Supply, op. cit.,* pp. 71, 72.

Chapter Six

1. Productivity Team Report, *Iron and Steel, op. cit.,* p. 20.
2. Productivity Team Report, *Steel Founding, op. cit.,* pp. 38, 39.
3. *Something Has Been Done,* Anglo-American Council on Productivity (U. K. Section), London, April 1952, p. 3.
4. *Ibid.,* p. 4.
5. *Productivity Conference,* 1952, British Steel Founders Association, London, p. 10.
6. *Ibid.,* p. 13.
7. *Ibid.,* p. 67.
8. *Ibid.,* p. 20.
9. *Ibid.,* p. 9.
10. Productivity Team Report, *Steel Construction, op. cit.,* p. 63.
11. Productivity Team Report, *Diesel Locomotives, op. cit.,* p. 35.

12. *Diesel Locomotive Industry*, The British Productivity Council, London, 1954, p. 7.
13. Productivity Team Report, *Building*, *op. cit.*, p. 65.
14. Productivity Team Report, *Electricity Supply*, *op. cit.*, pp. 65, 67, 69.
15. Productivity Team Report, *Letterpress Printing*, *op. cit.*, p. 56.
16. *Printing Industry*, The British Productivity Council, London, 1953, p. 5.
17. *Ibid.*, p. 4.
18. *Ibid.*, p. 8.
19. Productivity Team Report, *Cakes and Biscuits*, *op. cit.*, p. 46.
20. Productivity Team Report, *Cotton Spinning*, *op. cit.*, p. 5.
21. Productivity Team Report, *Men's Clothing*, *op. cit.*, p. 32.
22. Productivity Team Report, *Hosiery*, *op. cit.*, p. 10.
23. Productivity Team Report, *Footwear*, *op. cit.*, p. 16.
24. *Footwear Industry*, The British Productivity Council, London, 1953, p. 19.
25. *British Record*, British Information Service, New York, Sept. 16, 1954, p. 4.
26. *Footwear Industry*, *op. cit.*, p. 2.
27. *Trade Unions and Productivity*, British Trades Union Congress, *op. cit.*, p. 60.
28. *British Record*, *op. cit.*, April 30, 1953, p. 2.
29. Gray, A. P. and Abrams, Mark, *Construction of Esso Refinery, Fawley*, British Institute of Management, London, March, 1954, pp. 25–38.
30. *Progress Report*, The British Productivity Council, 1953–1954, London, 1954, p. 7.
31. *Ibid.*, p. 10.
32. *Productivity Conference*, 1952, British Steel Founders' Association, *op. cit.*, p. 9.
33. *Labor and Industry in Britain*, British Information Services, New York, Vol. XI, No. 4, Dec. 1953, p. 159.
34. *The New York Times*, Nov. 5, 1954.

Chapter Seven

1. *Analysis of Team Reports of Anglo-American Council*, (Chart) British Productivity Council, London, 1953.
2. *Ibid.*
3. *Ibid.*
4. *Labor and Management in a Common Enterprise*, Dorothea de Schweinitz, Harvard University Press, 1949, p. 37.
5. *Analysis of Team Reports of Anglo-American Council* (Chart), *op. cit.*
6. *Ibid.*
7. *Ibid.*
8. *Ibid.*
9. *Ibid.*

10. *Ibid.*
11. *Ibid.*
12. "The Productivity Reports," reprint from *Future*, London, June–July, 1951, p. 4.
13. Productivity Team Report, *Materials Handling, op. cit.,* p. 11.
14. "The Productivity Reports," *op. cit.,* p. 4.
15. Productivity Team Report, *Welding, op. cit.,* p. 53.
16. *Trade Unions and Productivity, op. cit.,* p. 59.
17. *British Record,* Sept. 16, 1954, *op. cit.,* p. 4.
18. *Analysis of Team Reports of Anglo-American* (Chart), *op. cit.*
19. *Summary of Work Done by Members of the E. C. A. Trade Union Technical Mission to the U. S.,* Harry L. Matthews, Sept. 29, 1951, p. 10 (mimeographed).
20. *Analysis of Team Reports of Anglo-American Council, op. cit.*
21. *Ibid.*
22. *Ibid.*
23. U. S. Productivity Team Report, *The British Pressed Metal Industry,* British Productivity Council, London, 1953, p. 25.
24. *British Record,* Oct. 29, 1954, *op. cit.,* p. 2.
25. *Ibid.*
26. *New York Times,* January 1, 1955.
27. *Analysis of Team Reports of Anglo-American Council, op. cit.*
28. *Profit Sharing,* Kenneth M. Thompson, Harper & Bros., 1947, p. 14.
29. *Analysis of Team Reports of Anglo-American Council, op. cit.*
30. *The World Almanac,* 1955, N. Y. *World-Telegram,* New York, p. 320.
31. *Ibid.,* p. 764.
32. *New York Times,* January 1, 1955.
33. *Ibid.,* January 4, 1955.
34. *The 20th Century Capitalist Revolution,* A. A. Berle Jr., Harcourt, Brace & Co., New York, 1954, p. 37.
35. *British Record, op. cit.,* Dec. 21, 1954, p. 3.
36. *The World Almanac,* 1955, *op. cit.,* p. 86.

Index